DEPARTMENT OF THE TREASURY

ALCOHOL AND TOBACCO TAX AND TRADE BUREAU

2010
TTB COMPLIANCE SEMINAR
FOR
BONDED WINE PREMISES

TRADE INVESTIGATIONS DIVISION

TTB P 5120.001(02/2010)

Index

Contents of this packet are not to be used for commercial purposes ~ thank you.

Notes

TTB Contact List

Alcohol and Tobacco Tax and Trade Bureau   (202) 453-2000
1310 "G" St., NW; Washington, DC 20220

Advertising, Labeling and Formulation Division   (202)   453-2250
   Toll   Free: (866) 927-ALFD (2533)
Applications for Label ("COLA") and Formula Approvals should be sent
to ALFD at the address shown above in Washington, D.C.

Registration information for COLAs ON-LINE: (866) 927-ALFD (2533)

Regulations & Rulings Division   (202)   453-2265

International Trade Division   (202)   453-2260
   TTB National Revenue Center (NRC)
   Federal Office Building   (513) 684-3334
   550 Main Street, Room 8002   Toll Free: (877) 882-3277
   Cincinnati, OH 45202-3263
   ttbwine@ttb.gov

Applications, Correspondence and Operations Reports from Distilled Spirits Plants,
Breweries, Wineries, Tobacco Products Manufacturers, Wholesalers and Importers
should be sent to the NRC.

Registration information for PAY.GOV: (877)   882-3277

Excise Tax Returns should be sent to:
     TTB – Excise Tax
     P.O. Box 790353
     St. Louis, MO 63179-0353

Questions regarding laboratory matters should be directed to:
Compliance Laboratory, Walnut Creek, CA
   Telephone: (513) 684-3356   Fax: (202) 453-2758

Wine Trade & Technical Advisor Mari Kirrane   (513)   684-3289

Wine Industry Analyst Perky Ramroth   (513)   684-3287

TTB WEBSITE: www.ttb.gov

4

Trade Investigations Division
Bob Angelo, Director
Steve Taylor, Deputy Director
(202) 453-2272
1310 "G" St, Ste. 200W; Washington, DC 20220

Western I   Al   Pederson, District Director
(513) 684 2481
Central and Southern California, Nevada

Western II   Kenneth   Klein, District Director
(513) 684-2491
Alaska, Hawaii, Washington, Oregon, Northern California

Mountain District   Glen Tischler, District Director
(513) 684-2730
Idaho, Montana, North Dakota, South Dakota, Minnesota, Wyoming, Nebraska,
Iowa, Utah, Colorado, Kansas, Missouri, Arizona, New Mexico, Oklahoma, Texas

Midwest District   Jerry Cajka, District Director
(513) 684-3019
Wisconsin, Michigan, Illinois, Indiana, Ohio, Kentucky, West Virginia, Virginia

Northeast District   Steve Albrecht, District Director
(202) 453-3144
Maine, Vermont, New Hampshire, New York, Massachusetts, Pennsylvania,
Maryland, District of Columbia, Rhode Island, Connecticut, New Jersey, Delaware

Southeast District   Ginger   Davis, District Director
 (202) 453-3117
Arkansas, Louisiana, Mississippi, Alabama, Tennessee, Georgia, Florida, South
Carolina, North Carolina

Puerto Rico Operations   Lottie Cifuentes, District Director
(202) 453-3164
Puerto Rico

Federal Laws

Internal Revenue Code: Title 26 United States Code, Chapter 51
Federal Alcohol Administration Act: Title 27 United States Code, Chapters 6 and 8

🖰 The federal laws pertaining to the wine industry are found on TTB's website and may be down-loaded without cost:

http://www.ttb.gov/other/statutes.shtml

Federal Regulations

Title 27 – ALCOHOL, TOBACCO PRODUCTS AND FIREARMS

The wine industry is governed by numerous Federal Regulations. Members of the wine industry need to be familiar with the regulations which govern their industry.

The regulations are found in Title 27 of the Code of Federal Regulations. The primary parts which pertain to the wine industry are listed here:

Part 1	Basic permit requirements
Part 4	Labeling and advertising of wine
Part 6	Tied House
Part 8	Exclusive Outlets
Part 9	American Viticultural Areas
Part 10	Commercial Bribery
Part 11	Consignment Sales
Part 12	Foreign Nongeneric Names of Geographic Significance
Part 13	Labeling Proceedings
Part 16	Alcoholic beverage health warning statement
Part 24	Wine
Part 27	Importation of Distilled Spirits, Wine and Beer
Part 28	Exportation of Alcohol

🖰 The Federal Regulations related to the Wine Industry are found on TTB's website and may be down-loaded without cost:

http://www.ttb.gov/wine/wine_regs.shtml

📖 A bound copy of Title 27 may be purchased from the Government Printing Office:

http://bookstore.gpo.gov/
Toll-Free: 1-866-512-1800

6

We encourage you to familiarize yourself with the primary parts of the Federal Regulations that pertain to the Wine Industry.

Wine – 27 CFR Part 24

Subpart A	Scope
Subpart B	Definitions
Subpart C	Administrative and Miscellaneous Provisions
Subpart D	Establishment and Operations
Subpart E	Construction and Equipment
Subpart F	Production of Wine
Subpart G	Production of Effervescent Wine
Subpart H	Production of Special Natural Wine
Subpart I	Production of Agricultural Wine
Subpart J	Production of Other than Standard Wine
Subpart K	Spirits
Subpart L	Storage, Treatment and Finishing of Wine
Subpart M	Losses of Wine
Subpart N	Removal, Return and Receipt of Wine
Subpart O	Records and Reports

Basic Permit Requirements under the Federal Alcohol Administration Act – 27 CFR Part 1

Subpart A	Scope
Subpart B	Definitions
Subpart C	Basic Permits
Subpart D	Nonindustrial Use of Distilled Spirits and Wine
Subpart E	Bulk Sales and Bottling of Distilled Spirits

Labeling and Advertising of Wine – 27 CFR Part 4

Subpart A	Scope
Subpart B	Definitions
Subpart C	Standards of Identity for Wine
Subpart D	Labeling Requirements for Wine
Subpart E	Requirements for Withdrawal of Wine from Customs Custody
Subpart F	Requirements for Approval of Labels of Wine Domestically Bottled or Packed
Subpart G	Advertising of Wine
Subpart H	Standards of Fill for Wine
Subpart I	General Provisions
Subpart J	American Grape Variety Names
Subpart K	Use of the Term "Organic"

Wine Premises Applications and Amendments

After starting business as a bonded winery or bonded wine cellar, you may need to notify TTB about changes among the people who own or control your company, or about the business you conduct, or changes you wish to make at the wine premises. The forms you will need to submit for each type of change are listed below.

📖 27 CFR Part 1; 27 CFR Part 24

Original Establishment

Original Qualification
Application to Establish and Operate Wine Premises Form 5120.25
Application for Basic Permit Form 5100.24 (not required for storage only)
Wine Bond Form 5120.36
Environmental Forms 5000.29 and 5000.30
Evidence of Signature Authority, if necessary
Statement that trade names were registered
Application for EIN, SS-4, if necessary
Organizational Documents, if necessary

Personnel / Ownership Changes

Change of Proprietorship
New owner files all "Original Qualification" documents.
Old owner files all "Termination" documents, listed below.

Change of Corporate Officers and Directors
Permittees: Immediate filing of Form 5100.18 and Amended Form 5120.25.
Non-Permittees: Amended Form 5120.25 and Form 5000.9 within 30 days of change.
Filing requirement for non-permittees may be waived by TTB for change of certain officers not directly involved in wine premises operations. See 27 CFR 24.124.

Partnership Changes: Change of General Partners - Same as Original Qualification

Limited Partnerships: Change of General Partners – Same as Original Qualification; Change of Limited Partners – Form 5100.18 and amended Form 5120.25, if +10% interest held

Limited Liability Companies: Changes in Managing Member or Controlling Interest – Same as Original Qualification
Change in Member(s) – Form 5100.18 and amended Form 5120.25

Change of Stockholders holding more than 10% of voting stock
Permittees: Immediate filing of Form 5100.18 and amended Form 5120.25
Non-Permittees: Amended Form 5120.25 with 30 days of change or letter notice annually on May 1 in accordance with 27 CFR 24.123; Form 5000.9

Change of Stock Control
Letter notice, filed immediately; Current Permit, surrendered for termination; Application Forms 5100.24 and 5120.25 within 30 days of change

Changes at the Premises

Change in Location
Amended Form 5120.25   Current Permit Surrendered
Form 5100.18 to amend permit   Environmental Forms 5000.29 and 5000.30
Superseding Bond Form 5120.36 or Consent of Surety Form 5000.18

Change of Address by the Post Office
Amended Form 5120.25
Current Permit surrendered; Form 5100.18 to amend permit

Change of Mailing Address
Form 5100.18 to amend permit

Change in Construction or Use of Buildings, including Ext./Curt. Of Premises
Letter to Director, National Revenue Center
Amended (updated) Form 5120.25 when next required for some other purpose

Establishment of Taxpaid Premises
Amended (updated) Form 5120.25

Non-Contiguous Extension of Premises
Amended Form 5120.25
Consent of Surety Form 5000.18
Environmental Forms 5000.29 and 5000.30

Alternation of Premises
Application Form 5120.25 with description of new operations
Consent of Surety Form 5000.18
Original Brewery, Distilled Spirits Plant, and/or Taxpaid Wine Bottling House application
Diagram

Alternation of Proprietors
Amended Form 5120.25 from Original Proprietor to depict alternation with the new Alternating Proprietor
Complete Wine Premises qualification packet from new Alternating Proprietor
Diagrams from Original and Alternating Proprietors
Copy of contract between Original and Alternating Proprietors may be requested

Name Changes

Addition of Trade Name
Letter Application or   Letter
Form 5100.18 with statement re: name of account
and registration
Form 5120.25 if not a permittee

Deletion of Trade Name
  Application or
Form 5100.18
Form 5120.25 if not a permittee

Change of Operating Name
Letter Application or Form 5100.18
Current Permit surrendered for amendment
Amended Form 5120.25

Other Changes

Signature Authority
Sole owners: Form 5000.8 for designated representative
Partnerships: Form 5000.8 for each partner and for representatives, as necessary
Corporations: Officers may be authorized as given in corporate minutes, resolutions, or on
Form 5100.1; Form 5000.8 for representatives, as necessary

Special Applications
Alternate method or procedure: Letter request
Modified form: Letter with sample of form

Change of Bond Amount
Strengthening or Superseding Bond Form 5120.36

Change of Bonding Company
Superseding Bond Form 5120.36
See List of Approved Sureties: http://www.fms.treas.gov/c570/index.html

Change of Bond from Cash Collateral to Surety Bond
Superseding Bond Form 5120.36

Change of Bond from Surety to Cash Collateral
Superseding Bond Form 5120.36
Cashier's Check or Money Order

Bankruptcy
a) Continuance of operations under a court appointed trustee:
   Trustee: File all documents listed under "Change in Proprietorship." Application must be
   approved before operations can continue.
   Proprietor: Notify TTB immediately and alert Trustee of Trustee's reporting requirements
   given in 27 CFR 24.125.

b) Discontinuance of operations as a result of bankruptcy:
   Proprietor files documents for "Termination."

Receivership

a) Wine premises taken over in receivership:
<u>Receiver:</u> File all documents listed under "Change in Proprietorship." Application must be approved before operations can continue.
<u>Proprietor:</u> Notify TTB immediately and alert Receiver of Receiver's reporting requirements given in 27 CFR 24.125.

b) Wine premises transferred to a new owner when it leaves receivership:
<u>Receiver:</u> File documents for "Termination."
<u>New owner:</u> File all documents listed under "Change in Proprietorship." Application must be approved before operations can continue.

Establishment of Bonded Wine Warehouse for Credit Purposes

Letter application from applicant in accordance with 27 CFR 24.108
Signed statement from proprietor of bonded wine premises
Consent of Surety

Termination

Letter Notice of Discontinuance
Current permit surrendered for termination
Final Report Form 5120.17
Final excise tax return Form 5000.24, as necessary
Certification that exports have been cleared, as necessary

☎ Who should I notify if I have any of these changes?

Please write or call your TTB Specialist at the National Revenue Center:

Alcohol and Tobacco Tax and Trade Bureau
Attn: Wine Applications Unit
550 Main Street, Room 8002
Cincinnati, OH 45202

Telephone: (513) 684-6882
Toll Free: (877) TTB-FAQS
E-Mail: ttbwine@ttb.gov
Fax: (513) 684-2226

Can I obtain the forms from the TTB website?

You can find all of the TTB forms listed above on our website:

http://www.ttb.gov/wine/forms.shtml

Application to Establish and Operate Wine Premises
Form 5120.25

This Internal Revenue Code application describes the physical layout of the bonded wine premises and the wine operations that will be conducted. Most of the questions about the premises and operations are listed on the back of the form, and should be answered on separate paper. All bonded wine premises must have an up-to-date Application Form 5120.25 on file with TTB.

OMB No. 1513-0009 (01/31/2013)

DEPARTMENT OF THE TREASURY
ALCOHOL AND TOBACCO TAX AND TRADE BUREAU (TTB)
APPLICATION TO ESTABLISH AND OPERATE WINE PREMISES
(See Instructions on next page)

1. SERIAL NUMBER
   1
2. DATE
   1/13/09
3. REGISTRY NUMBER *(Leave Blank if new applicant)*

4. TO: DIRECTOR, NATIONAL REVENUE CENTER
   ALCOHOL AND TOBACCO TAX AND TRADE BUREAU (TTB)
   550 Main St, Ste 8002 Cincinnati, OH 45202-5215

5. APPLICATION IS MADE TO OPERATE *(Check one only)*
   [✓] BONDED WINERY [ ] BONDED WINE CELLAR [ ] TAX PAID WINE BOTTLING HOUSE

6. NAME AND PRINCIPAL BUSINESS ADDRESS OF APPLICANT
   (Name and street, city, county, State, and ZIP Code)
   Linda K. Freeman and Frederick M. Johnstone
   HAZELNUT SPRING WINERY
   1191 Outlook Road
   Hazelnut Spring, CA 9xxxx

   PHONE # (xxx) 555-1000   EIN# 93-xxxxxxx

7. ADDRESS *(Address where wine operations will occur.)*
   (If different from address in Item 6)
   Same

   PHONE # Same

8. PURPOSE FOR WHICH FILED *(Such as original establishment, trade name change, alteration of premises)*

   Original: [✓] New Premises or Change in Proprietorship

   Amended for:
   [ ] Change in Location
   [ ] Change in information on application
   [ ] Change in Officers
   [ ] Change in Control (Date _/_/_)
   [ ] Change in Name of Proprietor or Trade Name

   [ ] Alternating Proprietorship with: _____
   [ ] Alternating Premises with _____
   [ ] Other: Please explain

9. APPLICATION FORM AND ATTACHED STATEMENTS AND DOCUMENTS SHOWING REQUIRED INFORMATION IN ITEMS 1-8 ON REVERSE OF FORM
   This application includes: (1) this form; (2) the papers and documents which are being submitted for the first time, and which are listed in Items 9A and 9B; (3) the current papers and documents from the latest approved TTB F 5120.25 Serial No. _____, which are listed in items 9A-1 and 9B-1; and (4) the supporting organizational documents filed in connection with another establishment but incorporated in this application by reference, and listed below in Item 9C.

9A. NUMBER OF PAGES ATTACHED TO THIS FORM ( ).
   PAGE NUMBERS   1, 2

9A-1. PAGES FROM CURRENT APPROVED TTB F 5120.25 THAT REMAIN CORRECT AND COMPLETE
   PAGE NUMBERS

9B. ORGANIZATIONAL DOCUMENTS SUBMITTED WITH THIS FORM *(List each document)*

   Partnership Agreement

9B-1. ORGANIZATIONAL DOCUMENTS FILED WITH PRIOR APPROVED TTB F 5120.25 *(List each document)*

9C. ORGANIZATIONAL DOCUMENTS FILED IN CONNECTION WITH ANOTHER ESTABLISHMENT BUT INCORPORATED IN THIS APPLICATION BY REFERENCE *(List each document, and show the name or plant number under which filed)*

NO WINE MAY BE PRODUCED OR UNTAXPAID WINE RECEIVED UNTIL THE PREMISES AND OPERATIONS ARE APPROVED BY THE DIRECTOR, NATIONAL REVENUE CENTER.

UNDER PENALTIES OF PERJURY, I DECLARE THAT I HAVE EXAMINED THIS APPLICATION AND, TO THE BEST OF MY KNOWLEDGE AND BELIEF, IT IS TRUE, CORRECT, AND COMPLETE.

10. SIGNATURE
   Linda K. Freeman

11. TITLE
   Partner

FOR TTB USE ONLY

APPLICATION IS: [ ] APPROVED   [ ] DISAPPROVED

EFFECTIVE DATE

SIGNATURE OF DIRECTOR, NATIONAL REVENUE CENTER

DATE

TTB F 5120.25 (01/2010)

Application Form 5120.25, continued: Answer the "Attached Statements and Documents" questions on a separate piece of paper (use as many as necessary). Number the pages, and attach the pages to the Application.

GENERAL INSTRUCTIONS

1. Each person desiring to conduct the operations of a bonded wine cellar, a bonded winery, or a taxpaid wine bottling house must file this application, in duplicate, with the Director, National Revenue Center, Alcohol and Tobacco Tax and Trade Bureau (TTB), at the address in Item 4.

2. The application information required will be on letter-sized paper with each attached page identified with the name of the applicant, the serial number of the application and the number of the page.

3. The proprietor is responsible for keeping information of an approved application current and complete. When required by 27 CFR Part 24, the proprietor must submit an amended application with supplemental or replacement pages or other documents necessary to update the previously approved application. Replacement pages must be numbered to correspond to the pages being replaced.

4. If this application is for a taxpaid wine bottling house, you will not conduct spirits operations or need a bond, so paragraphs 6 and 7 of the specific instructions are not applicable.

5. Applications must be submitted in accordance with the instructions on this form and in 27 CFR Part 24. Incomplete applications will be returned to the applicant without action.

SPECIFIC INSTRUCTIONS

Item 1. SERIAL NUMBER. Applications on this form must be serially numbered, commencing with serial number 1 for original establishment, and continuing in sequence for each subsequent application. Applications for a taxpaid wine bottling house will be filed separately and likewise begin with serial number 1.

Items 6 & 7. NAME AND ADDRESS. The address must be stated as explicitly as possible with a ZIP Code. If located in a city, the numbered street address and the name of the city will be given. If a rural address, give the name of the county and nearest post office, with the approximate distance and direction there from, including the name or number of the road or highway on which situated.

ATTACHED STATEMENTS AND DOCUMENTS

1. BUSINESS ORGANIZATION. If a statement is already on file with TTB for another authorization, only reference that authorization by name, address, and registry number per 27 CFR 24.105(k). Attach a statement, if not already on file, showing the type of business organization (e.g., sole owner, partnership, corporation, limited liability company) and the persons having an interest in the business supported by the following:

For corporations or limited liability companies:

   (a) Charter or certificate of existence, incorporation, or organization.
   (b) Names and addresses of officers, directors, members and managers.
   (c) Certified extracts of minutes authorizing certain individuals to sign.
   (d) Statement showing the number of shares/ownership of each class of stock/interest authorized and outstanding, and the voting rights of the respective owners or holders.
   (e) Statement of interest: Names and addresses of the 10 persons having the largest ownership or other interest and nature and amount of the stockholding or other interest of each, whether the interest appears in the name of the interested party or in the name of another party. The Director, National Revenue Center may request the names of interested persons if the applicant corporation or LLC is wholly owned or controlled by another corporation or LLC.

For partnerships:

   True copies of articles or partnership agreement, if any, and of the certificate of partnership where required to be filed by local authority.

2. WINE PREMISES. Describe each tract of land comprising the wine premises. Description must be by directions and distances, in feet and inches, with sufficient particularity to enable ready examination of the boundary of the wine premises. Describe the means employed to afford security of the wine premises. Describe where and how any taxpaid wine will be stored on the premises and the means used to segregate and identify taxpaid wine from untaxpaid wine. Describe any alternating areas. Each wine premises building must be described as to size, construction, and use. Buildings not used for the wine operations must be described only as to size and use. If wine premises consists of a partial building, rooms or floors, each must be described separately. Means of ingress and egress from the wine premises to adjoining portions must be described.

   (a) If operating a bonded winery or bonded wine cellar in a residential building, describe how the bonded premises are segregated from the residence and what direct access to the bonded premises is available.

   (b) If in an alternating proprietorship arrangement, provide a copy of the alternation agreement showing that each proprietor will conduct independent operations.

3. DISCLOSURE. If this application is not for a bonded wine premises in which production operations will be conducted and, thus a Federal Alcohol Administration Act basic permit is not required, would you agree to the listing of your name in a TTB publication which may be distributed to the general public upon request? A "no" response will have no effect on the consideration of this application. Under 26 U.S.C. 6103, you have a legal right not to give this release.

4. TRADE NAME. List each trade name to be used in connection with the wine operations. If State or local law requires registration, certify that each trade name is registered. State the operating name if other than the name in Item 6. If a trade name is listed in any basic permit issued, such trade name is not required to be included in this application.

5. SPIRITS OPERATIONS. Describe any operation which will involve the use of spirits.

6. BONDS AND PERMITS. With respect to this application, list all basic permits and bonds (including those filed with this application) showing the name and the surety for each bond.

7. VOLATILE FRUIT-FLAVOR CONCENTRATE OPERATIONS. For volatile fruit-flavor concentrate producers, submit a step-by-step description of the production process, commencing with obtaining the juice through each step of the process to removal of the concentrate from the system. For production of high-proof concentrate (more than 24 percent alcohol), indicate any step in the process at which the spirits are potable. Include the maximum quantity in gallons of fruit must and volatile fruit-flavor concentrate produced in 24 hours; the maximum and minimum fold; and the maximum percent of alcohol in the concentrate for each kind of fruit used.

8. OTHER OPERATIONS. Describe any other operations not specifically authorized by Part 24 that are to be conducted on the wine premises. This must include a list of the premises and any major equipment used, and a statement as to the relationship, if any, of the operation to the wine operations. These other operations need not be restricted to alcohol-related businesses.

PRIVACY ACT INFORMATION

The following information is provided pursuant to Section 3 of the Privacy Act of 1974 (5 U.S.C.§ 552a(e)(3)):

1. AUTHORITY. Solicitation of this information is made pursuant to 26 U.S.C. §5172. Disclosure of this information by the applicant is mandatory if the applicant wishes to obtain authorization for operating a bonded wine cellar, a bonded winery, or a taxpaid wine bottling house.

2. PURPOSE. To identify the applicant; to identify the nature, location, and the extent of the premises; the specific type or types of operations to be conducted on the premises; and to determine the eligibility of the applicant to register the wine premises.

3. ROUTINE USES. The information will be used by TTB to make determinations set forth in paragraph 2. In addition, the information may be disclosed to other Federal, State, foreign, and local law enforcement and regulatory agency personnel to verify information on the form where such disclosure is not prohibited by law. The information may further be disclosed to the Justice Department if it appears that the furnishing of false information may constitute a violation of Federal law. Finally, the information may be disclosed to members of the public in order to verify the information on the form where such disclosure is not prohibited by law.

4. EFFECTS OF NOT SUPPLYING REQUESTED INFORMATION. Failure to supply complete information will delay processing and may result in the denial of the application.

PAPERWORK REDUCTION ACT NOTICE

This request is in accordance with the Paperwork Reduction Act of 1995. This information collection is used by TTB to determine if the applicant is eligible to receive a wine premises permit. The information is required to obtain a benefit.

The estimated average burden associated with this collection of information is 15 minutes per respondent or recordkeeper, depending on individual circumstances. Comments concerning the accuracy of this burden estimate and suggestions for reducing this burden should be addressed to Reports Management Officer, Regulations and Rulings Division, Alcohol and Tobacco Tax and Trade Bureau, Washington, DC 20220.

An agency may not conduct or sponsor, and a person is not required to respond to, a collection of information unless it displays a current, valid OMB control number.

TTB F 5120.25 (01/2010)

Here is an example of how the "Attached Statements and Documents" questions on the back of Form 5120.25 can be answered:

Hazelnut Spring Winery - 1191 Outlook Road, Hazelnut Spring, CA 9xxxx
TTB Form 5120.25, S/N 1

1. <u>Business Organization</u>: This winery is a partnership, Linda K. Freeman and Frederick M. Johnstone, 50% - 50% partners.

2. <u>Wine Premises</u>: The wine premises is to be located on 30 acres of vineyard property owned by the partnership. The address is 1191 Outlook Road, Hazelnut Spring, CA 9xxxx. The property is approximately 4 miles north of the Hazelnut Spring Post Office, off Hwy. 2. The wine premises is at the end of the driveway; the point of commencement of the wine premises is the southeast corner of the building.

From the point of commencement, proceed west 90' to the southwest corner of the building, thence 180' north, thence 90' east, thence 180' south to the point of commencement. The entire building will be used for winery operations. There are no adjoining buildings.

One other building on the property is used for storage of agriculture equipment. It measures 110' by 70'. There is also the 1850 sf private residence of one of the partners.

The wine premises is a one-story building of wood construction with concrete floors. It is used for the production, bottling and storage of wine. There are two personnel doors, one near the southwest corner of the building, and one near the center of the north side of the building. There are six windows. All doors and windows are equipped for locking, and an alarm system is activated when the property is unoccupied.

With this application, we elect to establish the entire winery as Taxpaid Wine Premises. We will segregate taxpaid wine from untaxpaid wine, and will identify the taxpaid wine by affixing a sign on the cases or pallets which will prominently read, "TAXPAID."

We do not plan to alternate any parts of the premises at this time.

[Page 1]

---

3. <u>Disclosure:</u> Yes.

4. <u>Trade Names:</u> Additional trade names are listed on our application for a Basic Permit. They were registered with the County Clerk.

5. <u>Spirit Operations:</u> None.

6. <u>Bonds and Permits:</u> FAA Basic Permit is being applied for. Bond is TTB Form 5120.36, effective date 2/3/09 in the amount of $2,000.00. Surety is EverSafe Surety.

7. <u>Volatile Fruit-Flavor Concentrate Operations</u>: None.

8. <u>Other Operations</u>: None.

[Page 2]

When the information given on a previous application Form 5120.25 needs to be changed, submit a new cover sheet with the next serial number, and the attachment page(s) with the updated information. Here is an example of an amended application and attachment sheet:

OMB No. 1513-0009 (01/31/2013)

DEPARTMENT OF THE TREASURY	1. SERIAL NUMBER 2
ALCOHOL AND TOBACCO TAX AND TRADE BUREAU (TTB)	2. DATE 11/23/09
APPLICATION TO ESTABLISH AND OPERATE WINE PREMISES *(See instructions on next page)*	3. REGISTRY NUMBER (Leave Blank if new applicant) BWN-CA-16xxx

4. TO: DIRECTOR, NATIONAL REVENUE CENTER
ALCOHOL AND TOBACCO TAX AND TRADE BUREAU (TTB)
550 Main St, Ste 8002 Cincinnati, OH 45202-5215

5. APPLICATION IS MADE TO OPERATE *(Check one only)*
- [✓] BONDED WINERY
- [ ] BONDED WINE CELLAR
- [ ] TAX PAID WINE BOTTLING HOUSE

6. NAME AND PRINCIPAL BUSINESS ADDRESS OF APPLICANT
(Name and street, city, county, State, and ZIP Code)

Linda K. Freeman & Frederick M. Johnstone
HAZELNUT SPRING WINERY
1191 Outlook Road
Hazelnut Spring, CA 9xxxx

PHONE # (xxx) 555-1000   EIN# 93-xxxxxxx

7. ADDRESS (Address where wine operations will occur.)
(If different from address in Item 6)

Same

PHONE #

8. PURPOSE FOR WHICH FILED *(Such as original establishment, trade name change, alteration of premises)*

Original: [ ] New Premises or Change in Proprietorship

Amended for: [ ] Change in Location   [ ] Change in Control (Date _/_/_)
[ ] Change in information on application   [ ] Change in Name of Proprietor or Trade Name
[ ] Change in Officers

[ ] Alternating Proprietorship with: _____
[ ] Alternating Premises with _____
[✓] Other. Please explain Non-Contig. Extension of Premises

9. APPLICATION FORM AND ATTACHED STATEMENTS AND DOCUMENTS SHOWING REQUIRED INFORMATION IN ITEMS 1-8 ON REVERSE OF FORM
This application includes: (1) this form; (2) the papers and documents which are being submitted for the first time, and which are listed in Items 9A and 9B; (3) the current papers and documents from the latest approved TTB F 5120.25 Serial No. _____, which are listed in Items 9A-1 and 9B-1; and (4) the supporting organizational documents filed in connection with another establishment but incorporated in this application by reference, and listed below in Item 9C.

9A. NUMBER OF PAGES ATTACHED TO THIS FORM ( ).
1

PAGE NUMBERS 2

9A-1. PAGES FROM CURRENT APPROVED TTB F 5120.25 THAT REMAIN CORRECT AND COMPLETE

PAGE NUMBERS 1

9B. ORGANIZATIONAL DOCUMENTS SUBMITTED WITH THIS FORM *(List each document)*

9B-1. ORGANIZATIONAL DOCUMENTS FILED WITH PRIOR APPROVED TTB F 5120.25 *(List each document)*

Partnership Agreement

9C. ORGANIZATIONAL DOCUMENTS FILED IN CONNECTION WITH ANOTHER ESTABLISHMENT BUT INCORPORATED IN THIS APPLICATION BY REFERENCE *(List each document, and show the name or plant number under which filed)*

NO WINE MAY BE PRODUCED OR UNTAXPAID WINE RECEIVED UNTIL THE PREMISES AND OPERATIONS ARE APPROVED BY THE DIRECTOR, NATIONAL REVENUE CENTER.

UNDER PENALTIES OF PERJURY, I DECLARE THAT I HAVE EXAMINED THIS APPLICATION AND, TO THE BEST OF MY KNOWLEDGE AND BELIEF, IT IS TRUE, CORRECT, AND COMPLETE.

10. SIGNATURE *Linda K. Freeman*

11. TITLE Partner

FOR TTB USE ONLY

APPLICATION IS:
[ ] APPROVED   [ ] DISAPPROVED

EFFECTIVE DATE

SIGNATURE OF DIRECTOR, NATIONAL REVENUE CENTER

DATE

TTB F 5120.25 (01/2010)

Hazelnut Springs Winery - 1191 Outlook Road, Hazelnut Spring, CA 9xxxx
TTB Form 5120.25, S/N 2

2. <u>Wine Premises</u> (continued):

We are establishing with this application a non-contiguous extension of the bonded premises for barrel storage at 63 Middle Park Road, Hazelnut Spring, CA 9xxxx. The wine will return to the main winery for bottling. It is 1-½ miles from of the original wine premises and is owned by the partnership. The building measures 110' by 70'. It has one large sliding door and two windows, all of which are equipped for locking.   (new)

We do not plan to alternate any parts of the premises at this time.

3. <u>Disclosure</u>: Yes.

4. <u>Trade Names</u>: Additional trade names are listed on our application for a Basic Permit. They were registered with the County Clerk.

5. <u>Spirits Operations</u>: None.

6. <u>Bonds and Permits</u>: FAA Basic Permit Number is CA-W-15xxx. A superseding bond Form 5120.36, effective date 11/1/09 in the amount of $25,000 and a Consent of Surety to extend the terms of the bond to the non-contiguous warehouse are also being filed with this application. Surety is EverSafe Surety.   (Changed)

7. <u>Volatile Fruit-Flavor Concentrate Operations</u>: None.

8. <u>Other Operations</u>: None.

[Page 2]

Application for Basic Permit Under the FAA Act
Form 5100.24

Companies that produce and/or blend wine are required to obtain a Basic Permit under the Federal Alcohol Administration Act by submitting TTB Form 5100.24. Bonded wine premises which are established to store untaxpaid wine, but not produce or blend wine, are not required to obtain a Basic Permit.

OMB NO. 1513-0018 (08/31/2011)

DEPARTMENT OF THE TREASURY
ALCOHOL AND TOBACCO TAX AND TRADE BUREAU (TTB)
APPLICATION FOR BASIC PERMIT UNDER THE FEDERAL ALCOHOL ADMINISTRATION ACT

1. FULL NAME AND PREMISES ADDRESS
Linda K. Freeman & Frederick M. Johnstone
1191 Outlook Road, Hazelnut Spring, CA 9xxxx

TELEPHONE NUMBER
State in which organized for Corporations and Limited Liability Companies (LLC):

2. MAILING ADDRESS (If different from premises address)
Same

3. EMPLOYER IDENTIFICATION NUMBER (EIN)
(Social Security number is not acceptable)
93-99999xx

4. OPERATING NAME (DBA), if any
HAZELNUT SPRING WINERY

5. LABELING TRADE NAME(S), if any
Hazelnut Cellars; Nocciola Vineyards

6. BUSINESS(ES) TO BE CONDUCTED AT PREMISES ADDRESS (Check applicable boxes)

a. ☐ DISTILLED SPIRITS PLANT (BEVERAGE)
☐ DISTILLING
☐ WAREHOUSING AND BOTTLING DISTILLED SPIRITS
☐ PROCESSING (RECTIFYING) DISTILLED SPIRITS AND WINE

b. ☑ BONDED WINE PREMISES
☑ PRODUCING AND BLENDING WINE
☐ BLENDING WINE

c. ☐ IMPORTING INTO THE UNITED STATES
☐ DISTILLED SPIRITS
☐ WINE
☐ MALT BEVERAGES

d. ☐ PURCHASING FOR RESALE AT WHOLESALE
☐ DISTILLED SPIRITS
☐ WINE
☐ MALT BEVERAGES

or while so engaged, sell, offer, or deliver for sale, contract to sell, or ship in interstate or foreign commerce the alcoholic beverages so distilled, produced, rectified, blended or bottled, warehoused and bottled, imported, or purchased for resale at wholesale.

7. REASON FOR THE APPLICATION (use date format MM/DD/YYYY)

a. ☑ NEW BUSINESS
Anticipated start date 4/1/09

b. ☐ CHANGE IN CONTROL (Actual or legal)
☐ Submit Basic Permit(s) with this application
Date of Change _____

c. ☐ CHANGE IN OWNERSHIP
Date of Change _____
Name, address, and permit number(s) of predecessor

8. OWNER INFORMATION (List sole owner, all general parties, LLC members/managers, corporate officers and directors, and shareholders with more than 10% voting stock. Each listed person must also furnish the information in Item 9.)

NAME	TITLE	% VOTING/STOCK/INTEREST (If applicable)	INVESTMENT IN BUSINESS (Item 6)	SOURCE OF FUNDS INVESTED (savings, loans, gift, or specify other & financial institution name, city & state)
Linda K. Freeman	Partner	50%	$15,000	Savings
Frederick M. Johnstone	Partner	50%	$15,000	Sale of Stock

IF APPLICANT IS ACTUALLY OR LEGALLY CONTROLLED BY PERSONS OR BUSINESSES NOT IDENTIFIED ABOVE, PROVIDE ON A SEPARATE SHEET INFORMATION (as specified for Item 9) FOR EACH PERSON OR BUSINESS AND STATE THE EXTENT AND MANNER OF THE CONTROL. BUSINESSES SHOULD INCLUDE THEIR EIN.

9. COMPLETE FOR EACH PERSON LISTED IN ITEM 8.

a. FULL GIVEN NAME
Linda Kaye Freeman

b. DATE AND PLACE OF BIRTH
5/9/65 San Francisco, CA

c. SOCIAL SECURITY OR EMPLOYER IDENTIFICATION NUMBER
054-36-12xx

d. ARE YOU A U.S. CITIZEN?
☑ YES ☐ NO

e. ☐ MALE ☑ FEMALE

f. OTHER NAMES USED (Maiden name, nicknames, etc.)
none

g. RESIDENCE(S) OVER THE LAST FIVE YEARS
5/98 to present: 1191 Outlook Road, Hazelnut Spring, CA 9xxxx

TTB F 5100.24 (10/2008)   Page 1 of 2

18

a. FULL GIVEN NAME Frederick Martin Johnstone	b. DATE AND PLACE OF BIRTH 3/5/1970 Oakland, CA	c. SOCIAL SECURITY OR EMPLOYER IDENTIFICATION NUMBER 552-61-94xx	d. ARE YOU A U.S. CITIZEN? ☑ YES ☐ NO
e. ☑ MALE ☐ FEMALE	f. OTHER NAMES USED *(Maiden name, nicknames, etc.)* Marty Johnstone		
g. RESIDENCE(S) OVER THE LAST FIVE YEARS 7/99 to present: 2126 S. Valley View Road, Hazelnut Spring, CA 9xxxxx			

a. FULL GIVEN NAME	b. DATE AND PLACE OF BIRTH	c. SOCIAL SECURITY OR EMPLOYER IDENTIFICATION NUMBER	d. ARE YOU A U.S. CITIZEN? ☐ YES ☐ NO
e. ☐ MALE ☐ FEMALE	f. OTHER NAMES USED *(Maiden name, nicknames, etc.)*		
g. RESIDENCE(S) OVER THE LAST FIVE YEARS			

a. FULL GIVEN NAME	b. DATE AND PLACE OF BIRTH	c. SOCIAL SECURITY OR EMPLOYER IDENTIFICATION NUMBER	d. ARE YOU A U.S. CITIZEN? ☐ YES ☐ NO
e. ☐ MALE ☐ FEMALE	f. OTHER NAMES USED *(Maiden name, nicknames, etc.)*		
g. RESIDENCE(S) OVER THE LAST FIVE YEARS			

a. FULL GIVEN NAME	b. DATE AND PLACE OF BIRTH	c. SOCIAL SECURITY OR EMPLOYER IDENTIFICATION NUMBER	d. ARE YOU A U.S. CITIZEN? ☐ YES ☐ NO
e. ☐ MALE ☐ FEMALE	f. OTHER NAMES USED *(Maiden name, nicknames, etc.)*		
g. RESIDENCE(S) OVER THE LAST FIVE YEARS			

10. HAS THE APPLICANT OR ANY PERSON LISTED FOR ITEMS 8 OR 9 EVER BEEN DENIED A PERMIT, LICENSE, OR OTHER AUTHORIZATION TO ENGAGE IN ANY BUSINESS TO MANUFACTURE, DISTRIBUTE, IMPORT, SELL, OR USE ALCOHOL PRODUCTS *(beverage or nonbeverage)* BY ANY GOVERNMENT AGENCY *(Federal, State, local, or foreign)* OR HAD SUCH PERMIT, LICENSE, OR OTHER AUTHORIZATION REVOKED, SUSPENDED, OR OTHERWISE TERMINATED?

☐ YES. State details of each event on a separate sheet.　☑ NO

11. HAS THE APPLICANT OR ANY PERSON LISTED FOR ITEMS 8 OR 9 EVER BEEN ARRESTED FOR, CHARGED WITH, OR CONVICTED OF ANY CRIME UNDER FEDERAL, STATE, OR FOREIGN LAWS other than traffic violations or convictions that are not felonies under Federal or State law

☐ YES. State details of each event on a separate sheet.　☑ NO

TTB MAY REQUIRE additional information to process this application. If you are applying for a basic permit to operate a distilled spirits plant or bonded wine premises, you must also file additional forms and information required under the Internal Revenue Code. **OPERATION WITHOUT A PERMIT.** Criminal and administrative actions may be taken against persons engaged in a business listed in Item 6 of this form if it is not conducted pursuant to an FAA Act basic permit.

APPLICANT'S AFFIRMATION. Under penalties of perjury, I declare that I have examined this application, including accompanying statements, and to the best of my knowledge and belief, it is true, correct, and complete. The applicant must immediately notify the TTB official with whom this application is filed of any change in ownership, management, or control of the applicant *(in the case of a corporation, any change in the officers, directors, or persons holding 10 percent or more of the corporate stock)*. The business for which this application is made does not violate the law of the State in which the business will be conducted. In addition, if this application is approved, the applicant will conduct operations within a reasonable period of time and maintain such operations in conformity with Federal law.

12. APPLICANT'S SIGNATURE *(Sole owner, partner, corporate officer, LLC member or manager, or if designated agent, submit TTB F 5000.8)* *Linda K. Freeman*	13. TITLE OF PERSON SIGNING Partner	14. DATE 1/13/09
15. E-MAIL (INTERNET) ADDRESS *(optional)* Lindakaye@___.com		

TTB F 5100.24 (10/2008)

Page 2 of 2

INSTRUCTIONS

1. GENERAL. You must file this application if you want a permit under the Federal Alcohol Administration Act (FAA Act) to engage in the business of:

   - Producing or processing distilled spirits or wine includes for nonindustrial use.
   - Importing into the United States, or wholesaling, alcoholic beverages.

   Nonindustrial use of distilled spirits or wines includes all beverage purposes or uses in preparing foods or drinks. Wholesaling under the FAA Act means purchasing alcoholic beverages for resale at wholesale. The FAA Act defines alcoholic beverages as distilled spirits, wine, or malt beverages including any fermented cereal beverages which have an alcohol content of not less than 1/2 percent.

2. COMPLETING AND FILING THIS APPLICATION.

   - Please type or print and complete all items.
   - Write "not applicable" in any item requesting information that does not apply to your business.
   - Items 8 through 11: If this information is on file with TTB, state "On file under (name and TTB permit or registry number or type of pending application)."
   - If you need additional room, use a separate sheet.
   - If your producing or processing operations will be in Puerto Rico, contact the Director, Puerto Rico Operations, for additional requirements.
   - Send this form in duplicate to the appropriate TTB (Alcohol and Tobacco Tax and Trade Bureau) office.

Location of Business	Send to: TTB	
PUERTO RICO	Ste 310 Torre Chardon, 350 Carlos Chardon Ave San Juan, PR 00918 -21244	787-766-5584
ALL OTHER STATES	550 Main Street, Suite 8002 Cincinnati, OH 45202	1-877-882-3277

3. LABEL APPROVALS FOR BOTTLED ALCOHOLIC BEVERAGES. Bottlers, packagers, and importers should have TTB approved label certificates (TTB F 5100.31). A label approval is required to sell, ship, or deliver for sale or shipment, or to otherwise introduce in interstate or foreign commerce, alcoholic beverages. Also, a label approval allows importers to release specific imported alcoholic beverages from Customs' custody. For label approvals contact TTB, Advertising, Labeling and Formulation Division, Washington, DC 20220, (202-927-8140). TTB does not approve certificates until you have the appropriate FAA Act basic permit. You can submit draft labels (for example, mockups) to TTB for review before printing the labels. Trade name approval on your FAA Act basic permit does not constitute approval as a brand name for labeling purposes.

4. SPECIAL TAX. If you operate a distilled spirits plant or bonded wine premises or deal in beer, wine, or distilled spirits, file TTB F 5630.5, Special Tax Registration and Return, and pay an annual tax. File TTB F 5630.5 and pay this tax when you start selling, or offer for sale, alcoholic beverages. You do not file this form or pay special tax when your business only involves the importation or sale of fermented cereal beverages which have an alcoholic content of less than 1/2 percent or where your business is only in Puerto Rico.

5. EMPLOYER IDENTIFICATION NUMBER. You need to have this number for your business even if you do not have any employees. To obtain an EIN, file Form SS-4 with the Internal Revenue Service.

PRIVACY ACT INFORMATION

1. AUTHORITY. Solicitation of information on TTB F 5100.24 is made pursuant to 27 U.S.C. Section 204(c). Disclosure of this information by the applicant is mandatory if the applicant wishes to obtain a basic permit under the Federal Alcohol Administration Act.

2. PURPOSES. To identify the applicant, the location of the premises, and to determine the eligibility of the applicant to obtain a basic permit.

3. ROUTINE USES. The information will be used by TTB to make determinations set forth in paragraph 2 above. Where such disclosure is not prohibited, TTB officers may disclose this information to other Federal, State, foreign, and local law enforcement and regulatory agency personnel to verify information on the application, and for enforcement of the laws of such other agency. The information may be disclosed to the Justice Department if the application appears to be false or misleading. TTB officers may disclose the information to individuals to verify information on the application where such disclosure is not prohibited.

4. EFFECTS OF NOT SUPPLYING INFORMATION REQUESTED. TTB may delay or deny the issuance of the FAA Act basic permit where information is not complete or missing.

5. DISCLOSURE OF EMPLOYER IDENTIFICATION NUMBER AND SOCIAL SECURITY NUMBER. You do not have to supply these numbers. These numbers are used to identify an individual or business. If you do not supply the numbers, your application may be delayed.

PAPERWORK REDUCTION ACT NOTICE

This request is in accordance with the Paperwork Reduction of 1995. The information collection is used to determine the eligibility of the applicant to engage in certain operations, to determine the location and extent of operations, and to determine whether the operations will be in conformity with Federal laws and regulations. The information requested is required to obtain or retain a benefit and is mandatory by statute (27 U.S.C. 203 and 204 (c)).

The estimated average burden associated with this collection of information is 1 hour and 45 minutes per respondent depending on individual circumstances. Comments concerning the accuracy of this burden estimate and suggestions for reducing this burden should be addressed to Reports Management Officer, Regulations and Rulings Division, Alcohol and Tobacco Tax and Trade Bureau, Washington, DC 20220.

An agency may not conduct or sponsor, and a person is not required to respond to, a collection of information unless it displays a current, valid OMB control number.

TTB F 5100.24 (10/2008)

Application for Amended Basic Permit under the FAA Act
Form 5100.18

If the information originally submitted on Form 5100.24 needs to be corrected or changed, submit Form 5100.18 to the National Revenue Center for processing, along with the Basic Permit which needs correction.

OMB No. 1513-0019 (08/31/2011)

DEPARTMENT OF THE TREASURY
ALCOHOL AND TOBACCO TAX AND TRADE BUREAU (TTB)
APPLICATION FOR AMENDED BASIC PERMIT UNDER THE FEDERAL ALCOHOL ADMINISTRATION ACT
(See Instructions after this page)

1. NAME OF PERMITTEE Molto Bene Wines, Inc.	2. PERMIT NUMBER(S) TO BE AMENDED CA-W-15xxx (BWN-CA-156xx)	3. EMPLOYER IDENTIFICATION NUMBER 93-xxxx123

REASON FOR CHANGE

4. CHANGE NAME ON PERMIT		5. CHANGE OPERA-TIONS	CHANGE OPERATIONS ON PERMIT TO

6. CHANGE IN TRADE NAME(S)	ADD NEW TRADE NAME(S) *(State the purpose for which each trade name will be used. Use of trade name as a brand name on a label requires additional approval on TTB F 5100.31.)* D'Affonchio Cellars, for the account of D'Affonchio Vineyards. Name was registered with the County Clerk. REMOVE TRADE NAME(S)

7. CHANGE ADDRESS (ES)	CHANGE PREMISES ADDRESS TO *(Number, street, route, city or town, State, and ZIP Code)* CHANGE MAILING ADDRESS TO *(Number, street, route, city or town, State, and ZIP Code OR P.O. Box, city or town, State, and ZIP Code)*

8. CHANGE IN OFFICER, DIRECTOR, STOCK-HOLDER OR INVESTOR *(See instruction 1)*	REMOVE NAME

ADD THE FOLLOWING INDIVIDUAL *(Attach separate sheet if adding more than one person)*

a. FULL GIVEN NAME *(no initials)*	b. OTHER NAMES USED *(include maiden and married)*	c. ☐ MALE ☐ FEMALE

d. SOCIAL SECURITY NUMBER OR EMPLOYER IDENTIFICATION NUMBER	e. BIRTH DATE	f. PLACE OF BIRTH

g. ARE YOU A U.S. CITIZEN? ☐ YES ☐ NO	h. NUMBER AND TYPE OF SHARES HELD if person holds more than 10 percent.

i. TITLE WITH APPLICANT'S BUSINESS	j. INVESTMENT IN PERMITTEE'S BUSINESS if more than 10 percent of capital.	
k. RESIDENCES OR PRINCIPAL PLACES OF BUSINESS DURING THE PAST 5 YEARS	(1) NEW $	(2) SOURCE OF FUNDS *(examples, savings, loan, gift)*

l. HAS THIS PERSON EVER BEEN ARRESTED FOR, CHARGED WITH, OR CONVICTED OF, ANY CRIME UNDER FEDERAL, STATE, OR FOREIGN LAWS *other than misdemeanor traffic violations or convictions that are not felonies under Federal or State law?*
☐ YES *(State details of each event on a separate sheet.)* ☐ NO

m. HAS THIS PERSON EVER BEEN DENIED A PERMIT, LICENSE OR OTHER AUTHORIZATION TO ENGAGE IN ANY BUSINESS TO MANUFACTURE, DISTRIBUTE, IMPORT, SELL, OR USE ALCOHOL PRODUCTS *(beverage or nonbeverage)* BY ANY GOVERNMENT *(Federal, State, local, or foreign)* AGENCY OR HAD SUCH PERMIT, LICENSE, OR OTHER AUTHORIZATION REVOKED, SUSPENDED OR OTHERWISE TERMINATED?
☐ YES *(State the details on a separate sheet.)* ☐ NO

9. ADDITIONAL INFORMATION. TTB may require additional evidence necessary to verify this application.

10. PERMITTEE'S AFFIRMATION Under penalties of perjury, I declare that I have examined this application, including accompanying statements, and to the best of my knowledge and belief, it is true, correct, and complete. The business for which this permit is granted does not violate the law of the State in which business will be conducted.

11. SIGNATURE OF AUTHORIZED INDIVIDUAL *M. D. D'Affonchio*	12. TITLE President	13. TELEPHONE NO. (650) xxx-xx34	14. DATE 02/02/2009

15. E-MAIL (INTERNET) ADDRESS *(optional)*:

FOR TTB USE ONLY

16. SIGNATURE AND TITLE OF TTB OFFICIAL	17. DATE

TTB F 5100.18 (10/2008)

Request for Variance from Filing Certain Forms

Instead of completing Form 5100.18 each time you have a change to the Basic Permit, you may request permission to send a letter to TTB which describes the change. Here is an example of the letter which must be submitted and approved by TTB:

Name of Company
Address
Telephone Number

Date

Director, National Revenue Center   BW-XX-xxxx
Alcohol and Tobacco Tax and Trade Bureau   (XX-W-xxxx)
John Weld Peck Federal Bldg.
550 Main Street, Suite 8002
Cincinnati, OH 45202-3263

We request permission for a variance from regulations to file letterhead applications in lieu of amended notices, registrations or applications on TTB forms for routine changes such as:

Addition or deletion of trade name
Changes in corporate officers and directors

Thank you.

Sincerely yours,

(Name and title of person with signature authority)

Sample Trade Name Letter

Here is an example of a letter that may be submitted to TTB to report a change to the Basic Permit information, if your request for a variance from filing Form 5100.18 is approved:

Name of Company
Address
Telephone Number

Date

Director, National Revenue Center   BW-XX-xxxx
Alcohol and Tobacco Tax and Trade Bureau   (XX-W-xxxx)
John Weld Peck Federal Bldg.
550 Main Street, Suite 8002
Cincinnati, OH 45202-3263

Re: Trade Names

We wish to add the following trade name to our basic permit/registration:

Trade Name:

For the account of:

Registration Statement: This name was registered with the (xxxx) County Clerk's office on (date).

Permit and Registry Numbers: XX-W-xxxx; BW-XX-xxxx

We also wish to delete the trade name "xxxxx" from our permit, as we are no longer bottling with that name.

Sincerely yours,

(Name and title of person with signature authority)

Wine Bond Form 5120.36

All bonded wine premises must maintain bond coverage on Form 5120.36 which has sufficient operating and deferral coverage for the operations conducted at each premises.   The bond may be obtained through a Surety Company or by providing TTB-approved cash alternatives.

OMB No. 1513-0009 (01/31/2013)

DEPARTMENT OF THE TREASURY
ALCOHOL AND TOBACCO TAX AND TRADE BUREAU (TTB)
WINE BOND
(Submit duplicate originals. See additional instructions on page 3.)

REGISTRY NUMBER
(Leave blank if new applicant)

EFFECTIVE DATE

PRINCIPAL/OBLIGOR NAME AND PREMISES ADDRESS
(Number, Street, City, State, ZIP Code)

PRINCIPAL/OBLIGOR MAILING ADDRESS
(If different than Premises Address)

EIN:

BOND KIND (Select only one)

☐ ORIGINAL   ☐ STRENGTHENING   ☐ SUPERSEDING

BOND COVERAGE (Select applicable box(es))

☐ OPERATIONS $ _____   ☐ DEFERRAL $ _____   **TOTAL PENAL SUM* $ _____**

(Total Penal Sum equals OPERATIONS plus DEFERRAL Coverage on this bond. Deposited collateral must also equal Total Penal Sum.)
BOND CATEGORY (Select only one category (i.e. 'Surety,' 'Cash,' or 'Treasury Note/Bond') and complete corresponding items to right of selection.)

☐ SURETY: SURETY NAME _____   BOND NUMBER _____

☐ CASH: CHECK NUMBER(S) (i.e. personal check, cashier's check, money order, etc.) _____

☐ TREASURY NOTE/BOND**   TREASURY NOTE/BOND CUSIP NO. _____   TREASURY NOTE/BOND INTEREST RATE _____ %

TREASURY NOTE/BOND MATURITY DATE _____   TREASURY NOTE/BOND ISSUE DATE _____

** This bond is secured by the Treasury collateral (T-Note) described above or by a T-Note resulting from reinvestment of the full proceeds from the T-Note described above. T-Note collateral reinvestment automatically will occur upon maturity, unless the obligor notifies TTB in writing at least 45 days prior to the maturity date that the T-Note proceeds should not be reinvested and the obligor requests this bond be terminated.

Witness our hands and seals this _____ day of _____, 20___. Signed, sealed, and delivered in the presence of –

CORPORATIONS, PARTNERSHIPS, OR LLCs:
State in which principal/obligor organized: _____

Impress principal/obligor's corporate or LLC seal or check the checkbox below.

☐ The corporation/LLC has no seal.

Impress Surety Seal

Principal/Obligor Seal

By signing this document you acknowledge and agree to the terms and conditions described on page 2 of this form.

SURETY NAME

SURETY REPRESENTATIVE SIGNATURE

SURETY REPRESENTATIVE PRINTED NAME AND TITLE

PRINCIPAL/OBLIGOR NAME
BY:
PRINCIPAL/OBLIGOR REPRESENTATIVE SIGNATURE

PRINCIPAL/OBLIGOR REPRESENTATIVE PRINTED NAME AND TITLE

☐ Alterations made on this bond before and after execution were made with the consent of the Principal _____ and Surety _____ OR Obligor _____.

SIGNATURE, WITNESS 1 (if no seal)

SIGNATURE, WITNESS 2 (if no seal)

DIRECTOR, NATIONAL REVENUE CENTER APPROVAL: ON BEHALF OF THE UNITED STATES, I APPROVE THE FOREGOING BOND WHICH HAS BEEN EXECUTED IN DUE FORM IN COMPLIANCE WITH THE APPLICABLE LAWS, REGULATIONS, AND INSTRUCTIONS.

SIGNATURE OF AUTHORIZED OFFICIAL, ALCOHOL AND TOBACCO TAX AND TRADE BUREAU

DATE APPROVED

TTB F 5120.36 (01/2010) Previous Editions Obsolete   Page 1 of 3

24

PURPOSE: The above principal/obligor has filed an application to operate, or is operating, the bonded wine cellar or bonded winery specified.

DEFINITIONS: Definitions pertinent to this bond:

PRINCIPAL. The proprietor of the wine premises covered by a surety bond.

OBLIGOR. The proprietor of the wine premises covered by a collateral bond.

COLLATERAL BOND. A bond secured by tangible assets such as cash or United States Treasury Bond or Note.

CONDITIONS: The above principal/obligor and surety (sureties) are bound independently and jointly for payment to the United States in the above amount of lawful money of the United States. In this bond, the terms principal/obligor or surety include the heirs, executors, administrators, successors, and assigns of the principal/obligor or surety. Additional wine bond conditions are below. (If this bond covers only tax deferral, only the wine bond conditions in clauses 1, 2, and 3(a), and the Additional Wine Bond Conditions below will apply.)

BULK WINE WITHDRAWN FROM CUSTOMS CUSTODY: This bond covers the tax, for which the principal/obligor must become liable, on all wine withdrawn from customs custody in bulk containers and transferred to internal revenue bond at a bonded wine premises.

THE PRINCIPAL/OBLIGOR MUST:

(1) Comply with all requirements of law and regulations, now or hereafter in force, relating to the activities covered by this bond;

(2) Pay all penalties incurred and fines imposed for violations of law or regulations, now or hereafter in force, relating to the activities covered by this bond;

(3) Pay all taxes (including any penalties and interest in respect of failure to file a timely return or to pay such tax when due) on wine removed from bonded premises: Provided, that up to $500 of the operations coverage of a $1,000 bond ($1,000 operations coverage of a bond of $2,000 or more) may be applied to taxes that have been determined, but not paid on wine removed from bonded premises;

(4) Pay all taxes (including any penalties and interest) for which the principal/obligor may become liable with respect to the operation of the bonded wine premises, whether the transaction or operation on which liability is based occurred on or off the bonded wine premises, and on all wine, spirits, and volatile fruit-flavor concentrate, or any other commodity subject to tax under 26 U.S.C. Chapter 51, in transit to, or on the bonded wine premises;

(5) Comply with all requirements now or hereafter in force, pertaining to all wine or wine spirits received at, removed from, or returned to the bonded premises free of tax;

(6) With respect to wine withdrawn from the bonded wine premises without payment of tax as authorized by law (a) comply with all requirements of law and regulations,

now or hereafter in force relating thereto: and (b) as to the said wine or any part thereof withdrawn, for example, for exportation or for use on vessels or aircraft, or for transfer to a foreign-trade zone, or for transfer to a Customs Bonded Warehouse (CBW), and not exported, used or transferred, or otherwise lawfully disposed of or accounted for, pay the tax imposed thereon by law, now or hereafter in force, together with penalties and interest; and

(7) As the proprietor of an adjacent wine vinegar plant, pay all taxes, now or hereafter in force (including any penalties or interest), for which the principal/obligor may become liable with respect to the operation of the wine vinegar plant, and all wine now or hereafter in transit or on the premises of the wine vinegar plant.

ADDITIONAL WINE BOND CONDITIONS

CHANGE OF PREMISES: All stipulations, covenants, and agreements of this bond will extend to and apply to any change in the business address of the wine premises, the extension or curtailment of the premises, including the buildings thereon, or any equipment or any other change which requires the principal/obligor to file a new or amended application or notice, except where the change constitutes a change in the proprietorship of the business, or in the location of the premises. Further, this bond will continue in effect whenever operation of the wine premises is resumed from time to time following suspension of operations by an alternating proprietor.

TREASURY COLLATERAL BONDS: If this bond is filed as a collateral bond secured by a Treasury Note or Bond in an approved Department of the Treasury holding account, this bond is secured by the Treasury collateral identified on the face of the bond and any Treasury collateral resulting from rollover of the previous Treasury collateral. The Treasury collateral identified in this bond will automatically roll over upon maturity unless the obligor notifies the National Revenue Center at least 45 days prior to maturity.

DEFAULT: If the Principal/Obligor of a surety bond fails to fulfill any of the terms or conditions of this bond, the United States may seek compensation and pursue its remedies independently from either the principal/obligor or surety, or jointly from both. The surety hereby waives any right or privilege it may have of requiring, upon notice, or otherwise, that the United States will first commence action, intervene in any action of any nature whatsoever already commenced, or otherwise exhaust its remedies against the principal/obligor.

If the Obligor of a collateral bond fails to fulfill any of the terms or conditions of this bond, the United States may apply any outstanding tax liability (including any penalties or interest) against the collateral deposited.

EFFECTIVE DATE: If accepted by the United States, the bond will be effective according to its terms on and after the date without notice to the obligors. If no effective date is inserted in the space provided, the date of execution will be the effective date of the bond

INSTRUCTIONS

1. File duplicate **original** bonds with the Director, National Revenue Center, Alcohol and Tobacco Tax and Trade Bureau, 550 Main St, Ste 8002, Cincinnati, OH 45202-5215.

2. The name, including the full given name, of each party to the bond will be given in the heading, and each party must sign the bond with such party's signature, or the bond may be executed in the party's name by an empowered attorney-in-fact.

   a. In the case of a partnership, the partnership name, followed by the names of all its partners will be given in the heading. In executing the bond, the partnership name will be typed or written followed by the word "by" and the signatures of all partners, or the signature of any partner authorized to sign the bond for the firm, or the signature of an empowered attorney-in-fact. The name of the state in which the partnership is organized will be given in the space provided above the signature lines.

   b. If the principal/obligor is an LLC, the LLC name will be given in the heading. In executing the bond, the LLC name will be typed or written followed by the word "By" and the signature and title of the managing member, any member authorized to sign the bond for the LLC, or an empowered attorney-in-fact. The name of the state in which the LLC is organized will be given in the space provided above the signature lines.

   c. If the principal/obligor is a corporation, the heading will give the corporate name, the address of the principal business office, and the address of the premises. The name of the state in which the corporation is organized will be given in the space provided above the signature lines. The bond will be executed in the corporate name, immediately followed by the signature and title of the person authorized to act for the corporation.

   d. In the case of an individual owner as a sole proprietor, the proprietor's full given name will be given in the heading. In executing the bond, the proprietor's full given name will be typed or written followed by the signature, or the signature of an empowered attorney-in-fact.

3. If the bond is signed by an attorney-in-fact for the principal/obligor, or by one of the members of a partnership, LLC, or association, or by an officer or other person for a corporation, there will be filed with the bond an authenticated copy of the power of attorney, or resolution of the board of directors, or an excerpt of the bylaws, or other document, authorizing the person signing authorization has been previously filed with the Director, National Revenue Center, Alcohol and Tobacco Tax and Trade Bureau.

4. The signature for the surety will be attested under corporate seal. The signature for the principal/obligor, if a corporation or LLC, also will be attested by seal if the corporation or LLC has a seal. If the corporation or LLC has no seal, that fact will be noted. Each signature will be made in the presence of two persons (except where corporate or LLC seals are affixed), who must sign their names as witnesses.

5. A bond may be given with (a) corporate surety authorized to act as surety by the Secretary of the Treasury, (b) by the deposit of Government obligations. A Government obligation is defined in 31 U.S.C. 9301 as "a public debt obligation of the United States Government and an obligation whose principal and interest is unconditionally guaranteed by the Government." Such obligations include Treasury notes or Treasury bonds, or by cash in the form of a check or similar legal tender made payable to the Alcohol and Tobacco Tax and Trade Bureau for deposit in an approved Department of the Treasury holding account.

   Contact the National Revenue Center toll free at 1-877-882-3277 regarding allowable types of collateral.

6. If any alteration or erasure is made in the bond before or after its execution, check the box next to the alteration statement on page 1 and make sure that the Principal and Surety or Sureties **OR** Obligor initial the statement.

7. The penal sum named in the bond will be in accordance with 27 CFR Part 24.

8. If the bond is approved, a copy will be returned to the principal/obligor.

9. All correspondence about the filing of this form or any subsequent action, including termination, affecting this bond should be directed to the Director, National Revenue Center, Alcohol and Tobacco Tax and Trade Bureau, 550 Main St, Ste 8002, Cincinnati, OH 45202-5215 or 1-877-882-3277 (toll free).

PAPERWORK REDUCTION ACT NOTICE

This request is in accordance with the Paperwork Reduction Act of 1995. The information is used by the proprietor, or the proprietor and a surety company, as a contract to ensure tax payment. The information requested is required to obtain a benefit and is mandatory by statute (26 U.S.C. 5172).

The estimated average burden associated with this collection of information is 1 hour per respondent or recordkeeper, depending on individual circumstances. Comments concerning the accuracy of this burden estimate and suggestions for reducing this burden should be addressed to the Reports Management Officer, Regulations and Rulings Division, Alcohol and Tobacco Tax and Trade Bureau, Washington, DC 20220.

An agency may not conduct or sponsor, and a person is not required to respond to, a collection of information unless it displays a current, valid OMB control number.

TTB F 5120.36 (01/2010) Previous Editions Obsolete   Page 3 of 3

Wine Bond Instructions – TTB Form 5120.36

1. REGISTRY NUMBER: Assigned by TTB, BW/BWN/BWC _____ *(TTB will enter for original bonds).*

2. EFFECTIVE DATE: Date coverage will begin.

3. PRINCIPAL/OBLIGOR NAME AND PREMISES ADDRESS: Sole Owner enters his/her name and operating trade name, if any; partnership enters names of all partners and operating trade name, if any. Corporations and LLCs enter corporation's or LLC's name and operating trade name, if any. All Principal/Obligors must enter their premises address. Location of wine premises may differ from business/mailing address. If there is no street address, enter the physical location. Location of wine premises cannot be a Post Office Box.

4. PRINCI PAL/OBLIGOR MAILING ADDRESS: Business or mailing address; may differ from premises address. The mailing address may include a Post Office Box.

5. EIN: Employer Identification Number assigned by the Internal Revenue Service.

6. BOND KIND: "Original" – used only for new establishments or changes of ownership. "Strengthening" – increases the existing coverage. "Superseding" – replaces the existing coverage.

7. BO ND COVERAGE:

   - "Wine Operations" – covers tax liability of wine and wine spirits on hand and in transit to premises. Operations coverage is determined by used the "Bond Worksheet." Use the appropriate tax rate for the premises.
   - "Tax Deferral" – covers tax which has been determined, but not yet paid, on wine removed from the bonded premises for consumption or sale, provided that up to $500 of the operations coverage of a $1,000 bond and $1,000 of the operations coverage of a bond of $2,000 or more may be applied to taxes that have been determined, but not paid, on wine removed from the premises. If more than $1,000 Tax Deferral coverage is needed it can be shown in the Deferral dollar amount.
   - "Total Penal Sum" – Wine Operations plus additional Tax Deferral coverage on this bond.

8. BOND CATEGORY: (Select only one category and complete corresponding items to the right of selection.) Surety Company must be a federally approved surety. See list of approved sureties: http://www.fms.treas.gov/c570/c570.html#certified

9. Provide signatures as stated on Wine Bond TTB F 5120.36.

Evidence of Power of Attorney for Surety must be attached to <u>each Surety Bond</u>.

A surety bond must be signed correctly by the principals of the company operating the bonded wine premises and by the Surety Company. This page shows how the bond must be signed by Sole Proprietors, Partnerships, Limited Liability Companies and Corporations.

Sole Owners

Witness our hands and seals this _____ day of _____ 20 __ Signed, sealed and delivered in the presence of -

Impress Surety Seal

CORPORATIONS/PARTNERSHIPS, OR LLCs:
State in which principal/obligor organized: _____
Impress principal/obligor's corporate or LLC seal or check the checkbox below.
☐ The corporation/LLC has no seal.

By signing this document you acknowledge and agre to the terms and conditions described on page 2 of this form.

Surety Company Name
SURETY NAME

Surety Rep's Signature
SURETY REPRESENTATIVE SIGNATURE
Surety Rep's Name, Title
SURETY REPRESENTATIVE PRINTED NAME AND TITLE

☐ Alterations made on this bond before and after execution were mde with the consent of the Principal _____ and Surety _____ OR Obligor _____.

Company Name
PRINCIPAL/OBLIGOR NAME
BY: *Sole Owner's Signature*
PRINCIPAL/OBLIGOR REPRESENTATIVE SIGNATURE
Sole Owner's Name, Sole Owner
PRINCIPAL/OBLIGOR REPRESENTATIVE NAME AND TITLE
Witness #1's Signature
SIGNATURE, WITNESS 1 *(if no seal)*
Witness #2's Signature
SIGNATURE, WITNESS 2 *(if no seal)*

Partnerships

Witness our hands and seals this _____ day of _____ 20 __ Signed, sealed and delivered in the presence of -

Impress Surety Seal

CORPORATIONS/PARTNERSHIPS, OR LLCs:
State in which principal/obligor organized: _____
Impress principal/obligor's corporate or LLC seal or check the checkbox below.
☐ The corporation/LLC has no seal.

By signing this document you acknowledge and agre to the terms and conditions described on page 2 of this form.

Surety Company Name
SURETY NAME

Surety Rep's Signature
SURETY REPRESENTATIVE SIGNATURE
Surety Rep's Name, Title
SURETY REPRESENTATIVE PRINTED NAME AND TITLE

☐ Alterations made on this bond before and after execution were mde with the consent of the Principal _____ and Surety _____ OR Obligor _____.

Company Name
PRINCIPAL/OBLIGOR NAME
BY: *Partner's Signature*
PRINCIPAL/OBLIGOR REPRESENTATIVE SIGNATURE
Partner's Name, Partner
PRINCIPAL/OBLIGOR REPRESENTATIVE NAME AND TITLE
Witness #1's Signature
SIGNATURE, WITNESS 1 *(if no seal)*
Witness #2's Signature
SIGNATURE, WITNESS 2 *(if no seal)*

Limited Liability Companies

Witness our hands and seals this _____ day of _____ 20 __ Signed, sealed and delivered in the presence of -

Impress Surety Seal

CORPORATIONS/PARTNERSHIPS, OR LLCs:
State in which principal/obligor organized: _____
Impress principal/obligor's corporate or LLC seal or check the checkbox below.
☐ The corporation/LLC has no seal.

LLC's Seal

By signing this document you acknowledge and agre to the terms and conditions described on page 2 of this form.

Surety Company Name
SURETY NAME

Surety Rep's Signature
SURETY REPRESENTATIVE SIGNATURE
Surety Rep's Name, Title
SURETY REPRESENTATIVE PRINTED NAME AND TITLE

☐ Alterations made on this bond before and after execution were mde with the consent of the Principal _____ and Surety _____ OR Obligor _____.

Company Name
PRINCIPAL/OBLIGOR NAME
BY: *LLC Rep's Signature*
PRINCIPAL/OBLIGOR REPRESENTATIVE SIGNATURE
LLC Rep's Name, Title
PRINCIPAL/OBLIGOR REPRESENTATIVE NAME AND TITLE

SIGNATURE, WITNESS 1 *(if no seal)*

SIGNATURE, WITNESS 2 *(if no seal)*

Corporations

Witness our hands and seals this _____ day of _____ 20 __ Signed, sealed and delivered in the presence of -

Impress Surety Seal

CORPORATIONS/PARTNERSHIPS, OR LLCs:
State in which principal/obligor organized: _____
Impress principal/obligor's corporate or LLC seal or check the checkbox below.
☐ The corporation/LLC has no seal.

Company's Corporate Seal

By signing this document you acknowledge and agre to the terms and conditions described on page 2 of this form.

Surety Company Name
SURETY NAME

Surety Rep's Signature
SURETY REPRESENTATIVE SIGNATURE
Surety Rep's Name, Title
SURETY REPRESENTATIVE PRINTED NAME AND TITLE

☐ Alterations made on this bond before and after execution were mde with the consent of the Principal _____ and Surety _____ OR Obligor _____.

Company Name
PRINCIPAL/OBLIGOR NAME
BY: *Corporation Rep's Signature*
PRINCIPAL/OBLIGOR REPRESENTATIVE SIGNATURE
Corporation Rep's Name, Title
PRINCIPAL/OBLIGOR REPRESENTATIVE NAME AND TITLE

SIGNATURE, WITNESS 1 *(if no seal)*

SIGNATURE, WITNESS 2 *(if no seal)*

Alternatives to Filing a Wine Bond Form 5120.36 with a Surety Company

Cash Collateral
- Wine Bond Form 5120.36
- Cashier's Check or Money Order for full amount of bond is held by U.S. Treasury Department as collateral
- No interest is accrued

Treasury Note
- Wine Bond Form 5120.36
- Purchased through a bank or broker, who transfers the Treasury Note to the Federal Reserve Bank.
- Treasury Note is held by Federal Reserve Bank as collateral
- Interest is electronically deposited into the company's bank account

Contact the National Revenue Center's Wine Application Unit for further information:

Alcohol and Tobacco Tax and Trade Bureau
550 Main Street, Room 8002, Attn: Wine Applications Unit
Cincinnati, OH 45202

Telephone: (513) 684-6882
Toll Free: (877) TTB-FAQS
E-Mail: ttbwine@ttb.gov
Fax: (513) 684-2226

Wine Bond Worksheet - TTB 5120.36

OPERATING BOND COVERAGE

TAX LIABILITY AREAS	Gallons of Wine						Proof Gallons of Spirits
	Not Over 14%	More than 14% but not over 21%	More than 21% but not over 24%	Artificially Carbonated	Sparkling	Hard Cider	
Bulk Inventory							
Bottled Inventory							
In Transit from Other Bonded Wineries or DSFs							
Withdrawn for Export but Not Yet Certified							
Unaccounted for							
Total Gallons							
Multiply by Applicable Tax Rate*	$ 1.07	$ 1.57	$ 3.15	$ 3.30	$ 3.40	$ 0.226	$ 13.50
Total Tax Liability	$	$	$	$	$	$	$

* If you are eligible to use the Small Domestic Wine Producer Credit, use the appropriate tax rates after applying the Credit. Full tax rates apply to bulk wine imported in bond

GRAND TOTAL OF TAX LIABILITY $ _____

Penal Sum of Operating Bonds (See 27 CFR 24.148)

Tax Liability	Penal Sum of Bond
$0 - $1,000	= $1,000 (minimum)
$1,001 - $49,999	= Amount of Liability
$50,000 - $250,000	= $50,000
$250,000 and above	= $100,000 (maximum)

Tax Classes	Tax Rates	Tax Per Gallon
Not over 14%		$ 1.07*
More than 14%, not over 21%		$ 1.57*
More than 21%, not over 24%		$ 3.15*
Artificially Carbonated		$ 3.30*
Sparkling		$ 3.40
Hard Cider		$ 0.226*

*A credit of up to $.90/gallon ($0.056 for hard cider) on the first 100,000 gallons taxably removed may be available for producers of not more than 250,000 gallons per calendar year. See 27 CFR 24.278.

TTB F 5120.36w (09/2007)

Operating Bond Penal Sum Requirements

If Liability is:	Operating Bond Amount is:
Less than $50,000	$1,000 – amount as needed
$50,000 - $250,000	$50,000
$250,000 and above	$100,000

Examples:

1) A small winery has 10,000 gallons of not over 14% alcohol wine, 7,500 gallons of over 14-21% alcohol wine, and a 60 gallon drum of 140° spirits.

The tax liability on the not over 14% wine for this small winery is $.17 per gallon, and $.67 per gallon on the over 14-21% wine.

Wine/Spirits	Tax Class	Tax Rate	Tax Liability
10,000 gallons	Not over 14%	$ .17/gallon	$1,700.00
7,500 gallons	Over 14-21%	$ .67/gallon	$5,025.00
84 proof gallons	Distilled Spirits	$13.50/proof gallons	$1,134.00
		Total Liability:	$7,859.00
		Bond Requirement:	Not less than $8,000.00

2) A large winery with more wine on hand and 6,000 gallons of 140° spirits has a much higher tax liability:

Wine/Spirits	Tax Class	Tax Rate	Tax Value
100,000 gallons	Not over 14%	$1.07/gallon $107,000.00	
75,000 gallons	Over 14-21%	$1.57/gallon $117,750.00	
8,400 proof gallons	Distilled Spirits	$13.50/proof gallon	$113,400.00
		Total Liability:	$338,150.00
		Bond Requirement:	$100,000.00

Determining Tax Deferral Bond Coverage
📖 27 CFR 24.146(b)

When wine is removed from the bonded wine premises for consumption or sale, and the tax has been determined but the tax has not yet been paid, the tax deferral bond coverage must be sufficient to cover the amount of tax that, at any time, has been determined but not yet paid.

Quarterly Filings: To determine if your tax deferral bond coverage is sufficient for Quarterly Excise Tax Returns, compare your current deferral bond coverage to the amount of excise tax you expect will be determined during the quarter in 2010.

EXAMPLE, using 2009 taxable removals for guidance:

Jan. 1 – March 31	Due April 14	$2,250
April 1-13	Outstanding liability	$ 500
Total	liability	$2,750
April 1-June 30	Due July 14	$5,000
July 1-13	Outstanding liability	$ 250
Total	liability	$5,250
July 1 – Sept. 30	Due October 14	$5,500
October 1-12	Outstanding liability	$1,000
Total	liability	$6,500
Oct. 1 – Dec. 31	Due January 14	$7,000
January 1-14	Outstanding liability	$ 500
Total	liability	**$7,500**

1) Taxable removals in October, November and December 2009 totaled $7,000.00.
2) Taxable removals during January 1-14, 2009 totaled $500.00.
3) Tax liability was at its highest from October 1-January 14 at $7,500.00

You expect your removals to be similar in 2010. Your deferral bond coverage may be not less than $7,500.00. (A $10,000 bond deferral bond would allow for growth.)

Annual Filings: To determine if the $500 or $1,000 tax deferral coverage provided on your bond is sufficient for annual excise tax filing, estimate the amount of excise tax you expect will be due during 2010. Remember that you may only file annually if your taxes will total less than $1,000 and you do not have additional bond coverage. If the $500 or $1,000 provided on the bond is not sufficient, you will need to file your tax returns either quarterly or bi-weekly.

Bi-Weekly Filings: To determine if your tax deferral bond coverage is sufficient, compare your current deferral bond coverage to the maximum amount of excise tax you estimate will be due during 2010. This determination requires estimating what will be due, but not paid, during a typical semi-monthly tax period and during the 14 days that follow, until the tax is paid.

EXAMPLE, using 2009 taxable removals for guidance:

March 1-15	Due March 27	$2,000	
March 16-29	Outstanding liability	$ 500	
	Total liability March 1-27	$2,500	
March 16-31	Due April 14	$5,000	
April 1-13	Outstanding liability	$ 500	
	Total liability March 16-April 14	$5,500	
April 1-15	Due April 29	$8,000	
April 16-27	Outstanding liability	$2,000	
	Total liability April 1-29	**$10,000**	**(High Point)**
April 16-30	Due May 14	$7,500	
May 1-14	Outstanding liability	$1,000	
	Total liability April 16–May 14	$8,500	

Any person who signs forms that are submitted to TTB, or who will speak with TTB on behalf of the company, must have written authority on file giving that person permission to do so. The form used to give an individual Signature Authority is Form 5000.8, Power of Attorney.

OMB No. 1513-0014 (10/31/09)

DEPARTMENT OF THE TREASURY
ALCOHOL AND TOBACCO TAX AND TRADE BUREAU (TTB)
POWER OF ATTORNEY
(Please read instructions before completing this form)

1. PRINCIPAL *(Name of Partnership, Corporation, Association, Estate, or Individual)*   Hazelnut Spring Winery

2. BUSINESS IN WHICH ENGAGED   Bonded Winery

3. ADDRESS *(Number, Street, City, State, ZIP Code)*, TELEPHONE NUMBER, AND E-MAIL ADDRESS

1191 Outlook Road, Hazelnut Spring, CA 9xxxx   Tel: (xxx) 555-1000   E-Mail: Lindakaye@____.com

4. TAXPAYER IDENTIFICATION NUMBER *(Employer Identification Number or Social Security Number)*   93-xxxxxxx

5. PERMIT NUMBER / REGISTRY NUMBER *(If applicable)*   CA-W-16xxx (BWN-CA-16xxx)

6. NAME AND TELEPHONE NUMBER OF APPOINTED ATTORNEY   IRIS BRISTONATE   Tel: (xxx) 555-1000

7. ADDRESS *(Number, Street, City, State, and ZIP Code)*   1191 Outlook Road, Hazelnut Spring, CA 9xxxx

8. The above named principal, engaged in the business shown, has appointed the above named attorney to: *(See Instruction 2)*

(a) Execute for him/her all applications, notices, bonds, tax returns, tax information disclosure authorizations, and other instruments, claims, offers in compromise, letters, writings, and papers, and to act for him/her in dealing with the Alcohol and Tobacco Tax and Trade Bureau (TTB) in connection with matters relating to the laws and regulations administered by it. The principal authorizes the attorney named above to receive on his/her behalf any and all notices, papers, and letters from the Alcohol and Tobacco Tax and Trade Bureau in connection with all such matters, and grants him/her full power and authority to do all that is essential in and about the premises, as duly as the principal could do if personally present, with full power of substitution and revocation. The principal hereby ratifies and confirms all that the attorney must lawfully do or cause to be by virtue of this appointment.

(b)

9. The power is to apply to the following. (If authority is restricted to a particular factory, plant, premises, etc., give name as: Distilled Spirits Plant, Tobacco Products Factory, Tobacco Export Warehouse, etc., and address and registry number; or, if a Wholesale Liquor Dealer, SDA, or Tax-Free Alcohol User; or if this Power of Attorney may be used for manufacturing or importing firearms or ammunition, etc., give permit number.)

10. SIGNATURE OF APPOINTED ATTORNEY   *Iris Bristonate*

EXECUTION *(See Instruction 3)*

11. SIGNATURE IF PRINCIPAL IS INDIVIDUAL *(Signature of Principal)*   DATE

12. SIGNATURE IF PRINCIPAL IS PARTNERSHIP, LIMITED LIABILITY PARTNERSHIP (LLP), ESTATE, CORPORATION, LIMITED LIABILITY COMPANY (LLC), OR ASSOCIATION.
Under penalties of perjury, I declare that I have the authority to execute this power of attorney on behalf of the principal.

13. Seal of Corporation, Association, or LLC (A corporation, association or LLC will impress their seal below if they have one. If there is no seal, provide a resolution by the board of directors or organizational/supporting documents that support your company not having a seal, if applicable)

Signature	Title	Date
Linda K. Freeman Partner		12/13/2009
F. M. Johnston Partner		12/13/2009
Signature	Title	Date
Signature	Title	Date

TTB F 5000.8 (11/2006)   Page 1 of 2

14. ACKNOWLEDGMENT, WITNESSING, OR DECLARATION (Complete 14a, 14b, or 14c)

14a. ACKNOWLEDGMENT	14b. WITNESSING
The above-named person(s) signing as or for the principal(s) appeared before me today and acknowledged this power of attorney as his/her/their voluntary act and deed. The notarial seal must be affixed unless a seal is not required under the laws of the state where the power of attorney is executed.	This power of attorney was signed by or for the principal(s) by a person or persons known to, and in the presence of, the two disinterested witnesses whose signatures appear below:

NOTARIAL SEAL (If required)	Signature of Notary or Other Officer		Signature of Witness _F. Wosbere_	Date 12/13/2009
	Date	Title	Signature of Witness _A. J. Feeley_	Date 12/13/2009

14c. DECLARATION by attorney, certified public accountant, or enrolled practitioner who is granted the power of attorney by this form.

I declare that I am aware of the regulations of 31 CFR Part 8, that I am not currently under suspension or disbarment from practice before the Alcohol and Tobacco Tax and Trade Bureau, and that I am currently: *(Check applicable box)*

☐ A member in good standing of the bar of the highest court of¹ _____

☐ Qualified to practice as a certified public accountant in¹ _____

_____
Printed Name

¹Insert Name of State, Possession, or District of Columbia

_____
Signature

FOR TTB USE ONLY

DATE RECEIVED FOR FILING	DISTRICT	RECEIVED BY *(Signature and Title)*
DATE RECEIVED FOR FILING	TTB OFFICE	RECEIVED BY *(Signature and Title)*

INSTRUCTIONS

1. GENERAL. This form is filed with each TTB office in which the appointed attorney is to represent the principal.

2. ITEM 8. A full power of attorney is granted by paragraph 8(a). The power of attorney may be limited or restricted by deleting all of paragraph 8(a) and listing the specific powers to be conferred in section 8(b).

3. EXECUTION. This form must be signed by or on behalf of the principal(s) as follows:

   (a) INDIVIDUAL by his or her completion of Item 11.

   (b) PARTNERSHIP, LIMITED LIABILITY PARTNERSHIP (LLP) by completion of item 12 by all partners, or one partner who attaches his/her authorization to act on behalf of all the partners unless this authorization is provided by State law.

   (c) CORPORATION or ASSOCIATION by completion of items 12 and 13, an officer, preferably the president, vice-president, or treasurer, must sign in item 12.

   (d) ESTATE by completion of item 12 by the executor or administrator and attaching other such documents as may be required by TTB.

   (e) LIMITED LIABILITY COMPANY (LLC) by completion of item 12 by all members or managers, or one member or manager who attaches his/her authorization to act on behalf of the LLC.

4. FILING. This form must be completed in duplicate, unless otherwise required, and submitted to the Director, National Revenue Center, 550 Main St, Ste. 8002, Cincinnati, OH 45202-5215. The original with any attachments will be retained by the Director, National Revenue Center, and all other copies will be returned to the principal. If the power of attorney is applicable to more than one business establishment, additional copies must be submitted for each.

The additional copies will be filed in the same manner as when the power of attorney relates to only one establishment or business. Copies reproduced by photographic process need not be certified as copies of the original.

5. ORIGINAL OF A RULING. The Alcohol and Tobacco Tax and Trade Bureau will give to an appointed attorney the original of a ruling concerning the principal about TTB matters if a statement is made to that effect in item 8(b).

6. REVOCATION. A power of attorney remains in effect until revoked by the principal in written notice to the Director, National Revenue Center.

7. RULES. All persons representing clients before the Alcohol and Tobacco Tax and Trade Bureau must comply with the regulations governing representation *(26 CFR Part 601 or those regulations as recodified in 27 CFR Part 71)* and any other applicable rules and statutes.

PAPERWORK REDUCTION ACT NOTICE

This request is in accordance with the Paperwork Reduction Act of 1995. The information collection is used by TTB to ensure that only duly authorized individuals are signing documents. The information is voluntary.

The estimated average burden associated with this collection of information is 30 minutes per respondent or recordkeeper, depending on individual circumstances. Comments concerning the accuracy of this burden estimate and suggestions for reducing this burden should be addressed to the Reports Management Officer, Regulations and Rulings Division, Alcohol and Tobacco Tax and Trade Bureau, Washington, DC 20220.

An agency may not conduct or sponsor, and a person is not required to respond to, a collection of information unless it displays a current, valid OMB control number.

TTB F 5000.8 (11/2006)

A corporation or LLC may elect to use Form 5100.1, Signing Authority for Corporate and LLC Officials, to authorize the holders of certain offices or titles to sign documents and to discuss business matters with TTB.

OMB No. 1513-0036 (11/30/2010)

DEPARTMENT OF THE TREASURY
ALCOHOL AND TOBACCO TAX AND TRADE BUREAU (TTB)
SIGNING AUTHORITY FOR CORPORATE AND LLC OFFICIALS

NAME AND COMPLETE ADDRESS OF CORPORATION OR LLC	COMPLETE APPLICABLE INFORMATION
Molto Delizioso, Inc., dba MOLTO DELIZIOSO VINEYARD AND WINERY 6789 Pavia Road Spinoff, CA 9x9xx	☐ CHECK IF YOU ARE A NEW APPLICANT REGISTRY/PERMIT NO. BWN-CA-164xx (CA-W-16xxx)

BOARD MEETING	DATE OF MEETING
☑ DIRECTORS ☐ TRUSTEES ☐ MANAGERS ☐ GOVERNORS	12/15/2009

THE FOLLOWING CORPORATE/LLC OFFICIALS, EMPLOYEES, OR INCUMBENTS OF THE OFFICES LISTED ARE AUTHORIZED TO SIGN, OR TO APPOINT PERSONS AUTHORIZED TO SIGN, ALL DOCUMENTS UNLESS OTHERWISE SPECIFIED, SUBMITTED ON THE CORPORATION/ LLC'S BEHALF TO THE ALCOHOL AND TOBACCO TAX AND TRADE BUREAU. OUTSIDE CONSULTANTS MAY NOT APPOINT OTHERS TO SIGN ON THE CORPORATION/LLC'S BEHALF.

President

Vice-President

Secretary-Treasurer

I certify that this is true and complete and that the above authorization was granted at the cited meeting of the board.

SIGNATURE	PRINTED NAME	CORPORATE/LLC SEAL
E.T. DaVino	E. T. DaVino	
TITLE	DATE	☐ NO SEAL
President	12/15/2009	(if no seal, attach a resolution or meeting minutes that support the authority(ies) identified above.)

INSTRUCTIONS

Prepare and submit to the Director, National Revenue Center, Alcohol and Tobacco Tax and Trade Bureau, in duplicate. Each copy must be signed in ink by a corporate/LLC official and be embossed with the corporate/LLC seal (if any). This form may be used to list the corporate/LLC officials, or employees (if any), who are authorized by the articles of incorporation, the bylaws, or the board of directors in adopted resolutions or motions, to act on behalf of the corporation or to sign its name. If the authorization to sign is granted by position title, rather than to specific individuals by name, a new authorization will not be needed each time a change of incumbent occurs. However, if you list an individual's name along with a title/position, the authority is limited to the period of time that the specific individual holds the specific title/position. If an individual or incumbent's authority is restricted to a certain area of expertise or specific documents, identify the limitation next to the designation. WHERE THE AUTHORIZATION IS NOT GRANTED BY THE ARTICLES OF INCORPORATION OR ORGANIZATION, THE BY-LAWS, OR ACTION BY THE BOARD OF DIRECTORS OR MANAGING MEMBERS, TTB F 5000.8, POWER OF ATTORNEY, MUST BE SUBMITTED.

PAPERWORK REDUCTION ACT NOTICE

This request is in accordance with the Paperwork Reduction Act of 1995. This information collection is used by TTB to ensure that only duly authorized individuals are signing documents. This information is voluntary. The estimated average burden associated with this collection of information is .25 hours per respondent or recordkeeper depending on individual circumstances. Comments concerning the accuracy of this burden estimate and suggestions for reducing this burden should be addressed to the Reports Management Officer, Regulations and Rulings Division, Alcohol and Tobacco Tax and Trade Bureau, Washington, DC 20220. An agency may not conduct or sponsor, and a person is not required to respond to, a collection of information unless it displays a current, valid OMB control number.

TTB F 5100.1 (12/2007)

Options for Entering the Wine Industry

"Stand Alone" Bonded Winery: Some people dream of owning their own winery and producing wine for sale. They will qualify with TTB as a Bonded Winery. This qualification (generally registration under the Internal Revenue Code and issuance of a Basic Permit) allows a specific entity (example: a corporation) to conduct a specific activity (example, producing wine) at a specific location (the given address).

Alternating Proprietor: Others would also like to make wine for commercial purposes, but are not interested in building or buying a winery of their own. These companies find that sharing a winery facility with other companies will suit their purposes, and will qualify with TTB as an Alternating Proprietor winery. Each alternating proprietor must separately qualify, just as a stand-alone winery does, including obtaining their own registration, basic permit and bond, and maintaining their own records. This alternating proprietorship qualification is also specific to an entity, activity and location.

Custom Crush Customer (Wholesaler): Still others have grapes or other winemaking materials that they would like to have made into wine, but would prefer that someone else make the wine for them. These companies are Custom Crush Clients, and will qualify as Wholesalers. The Bonded Wineries that produce the wine for the Wholesalers are known as "custom crushers." The winery produces the wine, obtains the label approval and pays taxes on the wine; the client receives fully finished, bottled, labeled wine on which the Federal excise tax has been paid.

Bonded Wine Cellar: Some companies will qualify with TTB as a Bonded Wine Cellar, which is a bonded storage warehouse established to store, blend, or bottle untaxpaid wine. (Note: The Internal Revenue Code identifies all premises where untaxpaid wine operations take place as "bonded wine cellars" and those premises where wine is produced as "bonded wineries." For the purposes of this list, the term "bonded wine cellar" is used to identify those premises which store, blend, or bottle untaxpaid wine, but do not produce wine.)

Alternation of Wine Premises as a Brewery, Distilled Spirits Plant and/or Taxpaid Wine Bottling House
27 CFR 24.135

If you wish to alternate the use of the bonded wine premises as a brewery, distilled spirits plant or taxpaid wine bottling house, you must submit the following:

- Amended Form 5120.25 with description of new operations
- Diagram of premises
- Consent of Surety Form 5000.18 to cover winery premises alternation
- Original Brewery, Distilled Spirits Plant, and/or TPWBH application

Alternation of Wine Premises as a Distilled Spirits Plant for Alcohol Reduction of Wine
http://www.ttb.gov/wine/reduction_wine.shtml

When a bonded winery proprietor wishes to reduce the ethyl alcohol content of wine, certain processes are authorized by wine regulation 27 CFR 24.248, *Processes Authorized for the Treatment of Wine, Juice, and Distilling Materials*. The approved processes include Reverse Osmosis, the Spinning Cone Column and osmotic transport.

Although these processes are used to facilitate the creation of a wine product, they must be conducted on Distilled Spirits Plant (DSP) premises. The wine may be transferred in bond to a DSP for processing and returned to the winery, or the winery proprietor may wish to have the process conducted at the winery facility.

If the alcohol reduction is to take place at the winery facility, the proprietor of the bonded winery must first qualify to alternate the use of bonded wine premises as a DSP. Once qualified to alternate the premises as both a winery and DSP, the alcohol reduction may be conducted on DSP bonded premises. When the process is completed, the space and equipment can revert to winery use.

For further information and the necessary applications, please contact either the Wine Unit or the Distilled Spirits Plant Unit of the National Revenue Center at (513) 684-3334, or their toll free number, 877-TTB-FAQS (1-877-882-3277).

DEPARTMENT OF THE TREASURY
Alcohol and Tobacco Tax and Trade Bureau

Industry Circular
Number: 2008-4
Date: August 18, 2008

Alternating Proprietors at Bonded Wine Premises

To: Wine Premises Proprietors and Other Concerned Parties

This Industry Circular supersedes TTB Industry Circular 2003–7.

This circular:

- Reminds proprietors of the Alcohol and Tobacco Tax and Trade Bureau (TTB) regulations covering alternating proprietors at bonded wine premises;

- Outlines standards that TTB applies with respect to the qualification and operation of alternating proprietors at bonded wine premises;

- Describes the differences between alternating proprietor arrangements and custom crush wine production arrangements;

- States TTB policy regarding issues affecting alternating proprietors, such as the small domestic wine producer tax credit, separation among proprietors, and independence of operations; and

- Discusses instances when alternating proprietor arrangements are not consistent with TTB guidelines.

REASON FOR ISSUANCE

We are issuing this circular to remind alternating proprietors of the regulatory requirements covering qualification and operation of alternating proprietors on winery premises. We want to ensure that alternating proprietors on winery premises fully understand TTB's requirements for appropriate independence and segregation of operations regarding alternating proprietors. Failure to abide by these requirements creates delays in the examination of applications at the National Revenue Center (NRC) and in the field and, in ongoing wine operations, may result in adverse findings by the NRC or the field. Most often these failures relate to certain aspects of alternating winery operations. Examples of such problems include the use of permits by persons who are not engaged in the business of producing wine, underpayment of tax due to misuse of the small domestic wine producer tax credit, and mislabeling of wine. In this circular, we provide guidance regarding the standards TTB applies for the establishment and continuing operation of alternating winery proprietors.

BACKGROUND

Section 7805 and Chapter 51 of the Internal Revenue Code of 1986 (26 U.S.C.) (the IRC) authorize the Secretary of the Treasury (the Secretary) to promulgate regulations and administer the tax and qualification requirements for producing wine, including the qualification requirements for the small domestic wine producer tax credit. Sections 103 through 106 and section 117 of the Federal Alcohol Administration Act (the FAA Act), 27 U.S.C. 203 – 206 and 211, authorize the Secretary to carry out the provisions of the FAA Act with respect to qualification of wine producers, blenders, and wholesalers, and to labeling of wine.

The Secretary has delegated to TTB the authority to administer these rules. TTB regulations in 27 CFR parts 1 and 4 cover the wine permit and labeling requirements under the FAA Act, and TTB regulations in 27 CFR part 24 cover the registry, bonding, production, removal, tax payment and tax credit requirements for wine under the IRC. In these regulations, TTB sets out qualification requirements, including those for qualifying alternating proprietors. In this circular, "we" and "us" refer to TTB.

1. ALTERNATING PROPRIETOR ARRANGEMENTS

An alternating proprietor arrangement consists of two or more persons or entities taking turns using the same space and equipment to produce wine. In almost all situations, an existing proprietor-owner of a bonded wine premises agrees to rent space and equipment to a new proprietor. Such an agreement allows existing wineries to use excess capacity and gives new entrants to the wine business an opportunity to begin on a small scale without investing in equipment. The existing and new proprietors are sometimes informally referred to as "hosts" and "tenants," respectively. In other situations, two or more persons make plans to establish independently operated bonded wine premises, mutually agreeing to alternate the use of space and equipment. In these latter arrangements, no proprietor functions as a "host" to the others because each has agreed to share responsibility more or less equally. The designation of one alternating proprietor as a "host" to the other(s) is not a TTB requirement and carries no responsibilities or privileges that differ from those of the other alternating proprietors.

These arrangements must be formally approved by TTB through an application and approval process. Anyone making wine for sale must qualify with us as proprietor of a bonded winery and register the premises with TTB. Winery premises may not be used by or shared with any other party unless the necessary alternation applications have been approved by TTB. Regulations governing alternating proprietor arrangements are contained in 27 CFR 24.136.

2. "CUSTOM CRUSH" ARRANGEMENTS

A "custom crush" arrangement involves an agreement or formal contract under which a customer pays a wine producer to produce wine to order, after which the customer markets the wine. It is not an alternating proprietor arrangement. In a custom crush arrangement, the wine producer is authorized by TTB to make wine and is entirely responsible for producing the wine and for all related processing steps and regulatory requirements, which may include tax payment (unless the wine is transferred in bond to other bonded wine premises for these activities). The customer has none of these responsibilities, even when the custom crush customer may be involved in business decisions made about the wine, such as its production style, the appearance of its label, etc. TTB holds the producer/bottler accountable, not the custom crush customer. Even if the customer owns the grapes used to produce the wine, TTB still treats the transfer of the finished wine from the producer to the customer as a sale of wine for compliance purposes.

3. DISTINCTIONS BETWEEN AN ALTERNATING PROPRIETOR ARRANGEMENT AND A CUSTOM CRUSH ARRANGEMENT

a. Qualification, permit, and registry status. A winery proprietor cannot transfer or lend its qualification or premises to another person. Each alternating proprietor must qualify independently as a bonded winery under part 24 and obtain a Federal basic permit under part 1 as a wine producer to conduct operations at a specific location. In a custom crush arrangement, only the wine producer must register as a bonded winery under part 24 and obtain a Federal basic permit under part 1 as a wine producer. A customer who intends to market wine to other dealers must qualify as a wholesaler under part 1.

40

b. ***Records and reports.*** In an alternating proprietor arrangement, each proprietor must comply with requirements in 27 CFR part 24, subpart O, by keeping records of its operations and by providing operational reports to TTB. In a custom crush arrangement, the wine producer and bottler are responsible for keeping required records of winery operations and providing operational reports of the winery activities. The customer must maintain records of receipt and disposition as a wholesaler under 27 CFR part 31.

c. ***Certificate of Label Approval.*** In all instances, the wine bottler must obtain from TTB approval of an application for a Certificate of Label Approval (COLA) before bottling the wine. Thus, when an alternating proprietor arrangement includes alternating the use of bottling equipment, each alternating proprietor using the bottling equipment must obtain its own COLA(s) for the wine it will bottle. In a custom crush arrangement, the wine bottler obtains any necessary COLA from TTB. The customer never obtains the COLA from TTB, because the customer is not the bottler of the wine.

d. ***Tax payment.*** The Federal wine excise tax is paid at the appropriate rate by the proprietor that removes the wine from bond for consumption or sale. The rate of tax is determined by the tax class of the wine removed. The tax may be reduced if the taxpayer is eligible for the small domestic wine producer tax credit. Each alternating proprietor must individually pay excise tax for wine removed from its premises, at the applicable rate for each proprietor, unless the wine is transferred in bond. On the other hand, in a custom crush arrangement, the customer for whom the wine is produced will receive the wine after the Federal tax has been paid. The customer may have arranged to compensate the taxpayer for tax and other expenses as part of the price paid for services pursuant to the custom crush agreement.

e. ***Small domestic wine producer tax credit.*** This credit applies to proprietors who produce wine, but do not produce more than 250,000 gallons of wine per year. The full credit of 90 cents per gallon on the first 100,000 gallons removed is available to a proprietor who produces not more than 150,000 gallons of wine per year. For proprietors with production of more than 150,000 and not more than 250,000 gallons, the credit is gradually phased out. A group of wineries under common control (referred to as a "controlled group") are treated as a single winery for purposes of determining eligibility for the credit.

In an alternating proprietor arrangement, each proprietor's tax credit is based on the volume of wine produced and removed in that calendar year by the proprietor. If an alternating proprietor is eligible for the small domestic wine producer tax credit, the credit can, in certain instances, be transferred to another bonded wine premises proprietor to use when the excise tax is paid on qualifying batches of wine. See 26 U.S.C. 5041(c)(6). In a custom crush arrangement, TTB takes into consideration the wine producer's entire production and removals, including wine produced for a customer. Wine that was produced and removed for a custom crush customer counts toward the wine producer's own production and removals when determining whether the small domestic wine producer tax credit can be used.

4. RELEVANT TERMS UNDER THIS INDUSTRY CIRCULAR

Alternating Proprietor Agreement — The written agreement between alternating proprietors.

Bonded Wine Premises — A facility registered under the IRC for the production, blending, cellar treatment, storage, bottling, or packing of untaxpaid wine. These include:

Bonded Winery (Registry designation BW or BWN) — A bonded wine premises where wine is produced. The proprietor of these premises must also have a permit under the FAA Act to produce wine; and

Bonded Wine Cellar (Registry designation BWC) — A bonded wine premises where untaxpaid wine operations other than production are conducted. Often, but not always, this is a storage warehouse for bulk and/or bottled wine. Bonded wine cellars are operated pursuant to approved IRC registry, but some bonded wine cellar proprietors obtain a permit under the FAA Act to blend, but not produce, wine, or a wholesale permit if the operations on the premises are limited to purchase and resale of wine without production or blending operations.

5. CONCERNS OF TTB

While some applications from prospective alternating proprietors at bonded wine premises are filed by individuals with plans to make wine, we are concerned that other applications are filed for reasons unrelated to making wine. Filers of those other applications may seek to qualify as alternating proprietors in order to obtain benefits afforded to wine producers, such as Federal tax credits, or the ability to operate a tasting room under State rules.

6. POLICY

We evaluate each application for bonded wine premises registry under an alternating proprietor arrangement. We also review the ongoing operations of previously approved alternating proprietors. We take these steps to ensure that the physical layout of the wine premises to be shared, the compliance and business history of each party, and the day to day operations do not, or will not, create difficulty in administration, jeopardy to the revenue, or deception of the consumer. If we find any of these problems, TTB will:

- not approve the application for registry,
- reevaluate the appropriateness of and need for the alternating proprietor winery qualification,
- direct existing proprietors to make changes to operations or premises,
- collect underpaid taxes, or
- take corrective action on labeling, as appropriate.

The TTB official authorized to approve applications for registry of wine premises, including those for alternating proprietor arrangements, is the Director, National Revenue Center (NRC). The Director, NRC, applies the requirements of 27 CFR 24.136 in evaluating applications to operate as alternating proprietors. For both proposed and existing operations, TTB uses the following guidelines to measure compliance with 27 CFR 24.136:

a. *Alternating proprietor agreements and the need for qualification.*

TTB reviews the need for a permit when we examine applications for and operations under winery qualifications. Such examination includes whether the arrangement is truly an alternating proprietorship or whether it is really a custom crush arrangement. Under 27 CFR 1.24(b), we may consider the applicant's business history and likelihood to commence operations in a reasonable period and maintain operations in conformity with Federal law as part of the qualification process; under 27 CFR 1.50, we are authorized to revoke a permit if the permittee has not engaged in operations for 2 years.

The Director, NRC, may require a copy of the agreement or contract between the alternating proprietors, a business plan, or other information in support of each application for registry to operate as an alternating proprietor. TTB considers the business history of each applicant, his or her plans for development of future winery assets, and the level of commitment to the business as evidenced by investment in vineyards or other permanent assets. We examine each agreement or contract to assess the involvement of both parties in the wine operations, as well as the independence of each party.

42

When we look at business history, we find in some cases that an applicant for registry as an alternating proprietor has been a custom crush customer of a winery. Other applicants may have purchased finished wine with custom labels from the winery. When a person with such a business history seeks to qualify as an alternating proprietor at the same premises where wine was being produced for that person on a custom crush or private label basis, TTB looks for actual or substantive changes in the arrangements between the wine producer and its former wholesale customer. If it is evident from our reading of the agreement or contract submitted that an alternating proprietor applicant plans to have most or all of its wine operations conducted by its former wine supplier, we may find that the applicant has no intention of conducting winery operations and is therefore not qualified for a permit under § 1.24(b).

Other indications that one party to an alternation is not, in fact, involved in wine operations and may not qualify for a wine producer's permit include:

- A business plan that is primarily to market wine with little or no involvement in the production of the wine,

- A contract that specifies that a party will simply receive juice, ferment it into wine, and then transfer the wine to another party who performs all remaining wine processing activities,

- A contract for alternation that is based on quantity of wine produced and not on rental of space and equipment, and

- An agreement that indicates an alternating proprietor will have minimal involvement in its own wine operations, for example, if the agreement or contract states that another company's employees will handle the production activities, records, reports, and tax filings.

Although applicants making the arrangements described above may not qualify as wine producers, they may qualify for wholesale permits to market wine purchased from a producer or blender.

b. Suitability of the premises for sharing; the importance of keeping the wines of each alternating proprietor segregated and identified.

When two or more proprietors share premises, there is a potential for difficulty in separating and identifying one proprietor's wine from that of another. TTB must be able to locate and identify cased goods, barrels, and tanks assigned to each alternating proprietor. The regulations covering alternating proprietors provide that "[a]ll operations in any area, building, floor, or room to be alternated will be completely finished and all wine, spirits, and other accountable materials will be removed from the alternated wine premises or transferred to the incoming proprietor. However, wine, spirits, and other accountable materials may be retained in locked tanks at wine premises to be alternated and remain in the custody of the outgoing proprietor" (27 CFR 24.136(b)). Further, TTB regulations for all wine premises authorize the appropriate TTB officer to require a proprietor to segregate operations "to the extent deemed necessary to prevent jeopardy to the revenue, to prevent confusion between operations," and for several other purposes (27 CFR 24.27).

TTB will not approve plans which suggest that the floor space occupied by an alternating proprietor's barrels or cased goods constitutes that proprietor's premises. In some premises, signage or other marks may be considered sufficient separation of one proprietor's wine from another's, but in other premises TTB may determine that physical segregation such as fencing is necessary to protect the revenue. TTB will continue to make this determination on a case-by-case basis. Additionally, TTB may require more identification or separation of alternating areas in previously approved operations if we find that the daily practices do not provide adequate control and protection of the revenue.

Untaxpaid wine of an alternating proprietor which cannot be stored in space specifically designated for that alternating proprietor must be taxpaid or transferred in bond to the bonded premises of another proprietor with sufficient storage space. The proprietor of the receiving premises is responsible for the recordkeeping and reporting of that wine while it is maintained on his/her premises. Proprietors should be aware of the potential label consequences of transferring wine in bond to another proprietor. For example, even if the wine remains in the same physical location, if the wine is transferred in bond to the custody of another proprietor, the producer would lose eligibility to label that wine with an "estate bottled" claim. See 27 CFR 4.26 for the rules on labeling an estate bottled wine.

c. Employing the services of another proprietor's staff:

The agreement or contract between the alternating proprietors may include the option to hire the services of another proprietor's production and office employees. We will look to factors of authority and control to make a determination whether the proprietor is running an independent bonded wine premises operation. The proprietor employing the services of another proprietor's workers must direct and be fully responsible for those things that are usual and customary for the production, bottling, and storage of wine (as applicable) and the managing of the business. The producing alternating proprietor must provide its contract employees with written direction in the form of work orders or similar documentation.

Recordkeeping and reporting requirements under our regulations apply to the person who has physical custody of the wine, and are not based on who has title or legal ownership. We expect all proprietors to be able to access their winery records and to knowledgeably discuss those records with TTB officers. Relinquishing authority for the official records to a contract employee will be considered inadequate control. Alternating proprietors are reminded that when compliance violations or additional liability are determined, the proprietor employing the staff, and not the individual staff members, will be cited for violations or assessed for underpayment of tax. If a proprietor maintains its records solely in the computer system of another proprietor or is required to allow another proprietor to access its records, TTB would consider those practices to be indications that the proprietor is not operating as an independent alternating proprietor.

d. Access to premises.

The agreement must allow all proprietors to have reasonable access to their respective permanent premises and to their wine. For practical purposes, requiring an alternating proprietor to give notice when trucks will be on the premises, for example, is acceptable, but such requirements must not unduly hinder the operations of another proprietor or of TTB officers conducting investigations or audits.

e. Changing the terms of an approved alternating proprietor arrangement.

In addition to the qualification and tax issues discussed above, we wish to remind proprietors that alternating proprietor arrangements are conducted under an approved alternation plan that describes the areas to be used by each proprietor when that proprietor is active. The proprietors may not change the terms of the alternation plan before obtaining TTB approval of an amended application for each proprietor.

f. Eligibility of alternating proprietors for small domestic wine producer tax credit.

If alternating proprietors are independent small producers, they may be eligible for the small domestic wine producer tax credit. TTB will examine alternating proprietor arrangements to see if the proprietors are independent or if they should be considered members of a controlled group. In the latter case, all proprietors' production and removal amounts will be combined for the purpose of determining whether credit may be used by the group. If applicable, a single small domestic wine producer tax credit will be apportioned among all participants.

Indications that alternating proprietors are not independent may include:

- A contract that allows one alternating proprietor to transfer "excess" custom crush business to another alternating proprietor;

- An observed pattern of operations in which an existing alternating proprietor annually produces a very small volume of wine in order to qualify as a small producer for tax credit purposes, and then has a large volume of wine produced for it on a custom crush basis by another winery; or

- Evidence that a producer encourages its customers to become alternating proprietors in order to split production.

TTB will deny the credit if it benefits a large producer and will ensure proper reduction of the credit for persons producing more than 150,000 gallons of wine during a calendar year.

g. Need for permanent premises.

TTB will consider approving a plan in which an alternating proprietor suspends and then resumes operations. A proprietor who does not anticipate conducting wine operations for an extended period and wishes to make the entire bonded premises available for use by another proprietor may request such a suspension of operations. In this event, before suspending its bonded wine premises operations, the outgoing proprietor is required to transfer in bond to another qualified bonded wine premises, or taxably remove, all wine on the premises. Under 27 CFR 24.35, each alternating proprietor must maintain its own winery records and make them available for TTB examination at the bonded wine premises. However, under 27 CFR 24.22, a proprietor may request permission to maintain the records at a separate and permanent business office address (but not at another proprietor's premises), where TTB may contact the proprietor and review records during business hours. When an applicant expresses a need to use bonded wine premises only on a very infrequent basis, however, TTB will thoroughly examine his or her need for qualification as a producer, rather than as a wholesaler/custom crush customer of the proprietor producing the wine.

h. Alternation for less than a day.

The regulations covering alternating proprietors provide that "[o]peration of a bonded winery engaged in the production of wine by an alternate proprietor will be at least one calendar day in length" (27 CFR 24.136(a)). A winery engages in the production of wine by fermenting juice, ameliorating wine, adding wine spirits to wine, sweetening wine, producing effervescent wine, or producing formula wine. Receiving and crushing grapes are not production for purposes of winery qualification. Specific extensions and curtailments of premises, such as use of a bottling line by an alternating proprietor, may be for less than a calendar day, as long as the extensions and curtailments are part of the approved alternation plan.

7. CONCLUSION

TTB recognizes that alternating proprietor arrangements may be undertaken for one or more valid reasons. We will continue to review proposed and existing alternating proprietor arrangements to ensure that the proprietors conduct independent operations and that those who take the small domestic wine producer tax credit are entitled to it. If we determine that a company is conducting alternating proprietor operations in a manner that is not independent, or in a manner that jeopardizes the revenue, or in a manner that results in mislabeling of wine, we will initiate corrective action, which could include, among other corrective action, revoking the alternation approval, revoking the basic permit, directing the proprietors to modify the premises, adjusting the taxes, or directing a proprietor to relabel wine.

QUESTIONS: If you have questions concerning this circular, contact the Regulations and Rulings Division, Alcohol and Tobacco Tax and Trade Bureau, 1310 G Street, NW, Washington, DC 20220.

John J. Manfreda
Administrator
Alcohol and Tobacco Tax and Trade Bureau

TTB Wine FAQ #11: What are the Federal Requirements for "Custom Crush" Clients and Winemakers?

http://www.ttb.gov/wine/faq.shtml#w11

In a typical custom crush arrangement, a grape grower or any person with winemaking materials (the "client") enters into a contract with a bonded winery proprietor to have the grapes processed into wine. The client retains title to the grapes, and the wine is made to the client's specifications. The finished wine is returned to the client for sale to other dealers, or the winery sometimes sells the wine on behalf of the client. TTB has received questions about the regulatory responsibilities of the custom crush client and the wine producer.

The custom crush client may be required to obtain a Federal Wholesaler's Basic Permit from TTB. This permit allows the client to engage in the business of purchasing wine for resale at wholesale, in accordance with the Federal Alcohol Administration Act at 27 U.S.C. 203(c)(1) and 27 CFR 1.22. Although the client is specifically paying for the producer's services, the client has purchased wine (within the broad meaning of the term) at the price set in the agreement. If the client engages in activities normally associated with wholesaling, such as setting the price for the wine, determining which dealers will be sold the wine, and controlling and paying for advertising of the product, the client must have a wholesaler's basic permit. If, however, the client merely receives the proceeds from the sale by the winery of the resulting wine, a permit would not be required.

In addition to the basic permit requirement, the custom crush client who engages in the business of selling wine must submit the Special Occupational Tax Registration Form 5630.8R as a wholesaler if the wine is offered for sale to other dealers, or as a retailer if the wine is only offered for sale to consumers.

Bonded winery proprietors must ensure that the receipt of winemaking materials and the ensuing activities associated with the production of custom crush wine is properly recorded. TTB reminds the industry that wine produced for custom crush clients carries the same regulatory requirements for recordkeeping, reporting, labeling and taxation as wine made for the winery itself.

The bottling winery is responsible for obtaining an appropriate Certificate of Label approval, and the wine premises which releases the wine to the client is responsible for payment of federal excise tax at the rate appropriate for the producing winery. For the purposes of determining eligibility for the Small Domestic Producer's Credit, all wine produced for clients must be included in the production and removal calculations (see 27 CFR 24.278-9).

#

TTB Wine FAQ #4: What are the Federal Guidelines for Home Winemakers' Centers?

http://www.ttb.gov/wine/faq.shtml#w4

The Alcohol and Tobacco Tax and Trade Bureau (TTB) has been asked if there are any Federal requirements covering operation of a Home Winemakers' Center. Home Winemakers' Centers are places where an individual pays a fee to use space and equipment to make wine for personal or family use.

Although we refer to the individual making wine for personal or family use as a "home winemaker," the wine may be made somewhere other than the individual's residence, including a Home Winemakers' Center. We find that a Home Winemakers' Center may operate without qualifying under federal rules as a bonded wine cellar or paying federal excise tax on wine produced at the Center by individuals under the following conditions:

Compliance with State and local law

The ability to produce wine for personal or family use and without payment of tax under Federal law does not authorize production of wine by individuals or operation of a Home Winemakers' Center in violation of State or local law. The operator of a Home Winemakers' Center must learn and comply with any permit, license or tax requirements of State and local law and conduct operations in compliance with State and local law.

Use by qualified individuals

The customers who make wine at the center must be qualified to produce wine for personal or family use under federal, State and local rules. If State and local rules impose different requirements or limitations than the federal rules noted here, the stricter rules and limits should be applied. Under Federal law, any adult may, without payment of tax, produce wine for personal or family use under regulations in 27 CFR 24.75, which provide the following:

- The individual must follow applicable State and local laws.
- The individual must be 18 years of age or the legal age to purchase wine in the locality whichever is older.
- The individual may produce, without payment of tax, per household, up to 100 gallons of wine per calendar year if there is one adult residing in the household, or 200 gallons if there are two or more adults residing in the household.
- The individual may remove wine from the place where it is made for personal or family use, including use in contests or tasting.
- The individual may not produce wine for sale or offer wine for sale.

Non-commercial use

The operations must never "cross the line" to commercial production or sale of wine. Proprietors and employees of Home Winemakers' Centers:

- May furnish space, equipment, ingredients, bottling supplies and advice to customers.
- May provide certain assistance to customers including:
  - Moving containers of wine between storage areas.
  - Cleaning, maintenance, and repair of equipment.
  - Climate and temperature control.
  - Disposal of wastes.
  - Quality control (including laboratory analysis and tasting of wine for quality control purposes).
- May not provide physical assistance to, or on behalf of, customers in the production, wine, add ingredients to wine, or provide other physical assistance in producing or bottling wine.
- May not provide non-tax paid wine to customers or prospective customers for sampling or other reasons.

Operation of a Home Winemakers' Center in a manner contrary to the conditions outlined may cause the facility to be considered a commercial winery, subject to all statutory and regulatory provisions relating to winery operation, including registry requirements and possible liability for back taxes.

Under some circumstances, a TTB qualified bonded wine cellar may operate a Home Winemakers' Center. All wine produced at a Home Winemakers' Center on wine premises is taxable under Federal law and is subject to other requirements.

For further information regarding qualification of a bonded wine premises or operation of a Home Winemakers' Center at bonded wine premises, contact:

The Alcohol and Tobacco Tax and Trade Bureau
National Revenue Center
550 Main Street, Cincinnati, OH 45202
Telephone (toll free) 877- 882-3277

TAXPAID REMOVALS

   The regulations pertaining to taxpaid removals of wine products are found in the Internal Revenue Code at 26 U.S.C. 5041 and in the Wine Regulations, 27 CFR 24.270-.279 and 27 CFR 24.310:

24.270 Determination of tax.
24.271 Payment of tax by check, cash, or money order.
24.272 Payment of tax by electronic fund transfer.
24.273 Exception to filing semi-monthly tax returns.
24.274 Failure to timely pay tax or file a return.
24.275 Prepayment of tax.
24.276 Prepayment of tax; proprietor in default.
24.277 Date of mailing or delivering of returns.
24.278 Tax credit for certain small domestic producers.
24.279 Tax adjustments related to wine credit.
24.310 Taxpaid removals from bond record.

http://www.ttb.gov/wine/wine_regs.shtml

Attachment, Determination, Payment

- The tax value of the wine is attached when the wine is produced. (26 U.S.C. 5041)

- The amount to be paid is determined when wine is removed from bonded premises for consumption or sale. (27 CFR 24.270)

- Wine excise tax is paid semi-monthly, quarterly or annually. (27 CFR 24.271, .273)

When is Wine "Produced?"

In accordance with wine regulation 27 CFR 24.176(b), wine is declared produced upon completion of fermentation or removal from the fermenter. At that point the volume of wine is to be accurately determined, recorded and reported on TTB Form 5120.17, Report of Wine Premises Operations, as wine produced. An alcohol test should be conducted to accurately determine the tax class of the wine.

Taxpaid Removals from Bond Record
27 CFR 24.310

When wine is removed from a bonded winery or bonded wine cellar for consumption or sale, a record must be kept which contains the information listed below. The Taxpaid Removals from Bond Record may be a compilation of source documents OR a summary record.

☐ Date of Removal

☐ The name and address of the person to whom removed; however, on any individual sale of less than 80 liters, the name and address of the purchaser need not be recorded

☐ The volume, kind (class and type), and alcohol content of the wine

☐ When removing taxpaid bulk wine to another wine premises, shipping record will be prepared in accordance with 27 CFR 24.281

☐ Volume of wine removed taxpaid will be <u>summarized daily</u> by tax class in wine gallons to the nearest tenth gallon

An invoice containing the information listed above is a common removal record.

Here is an example of an individual invoice that has all of the necessary information required for the Taxpaid Removals from Bond Record, 27 CFR 24.310. The amount removed from bond is extended to five decimal places on individual invoices. The total volume removed for the day is rounded to the nearest 10th of a gallon on a daily summary.

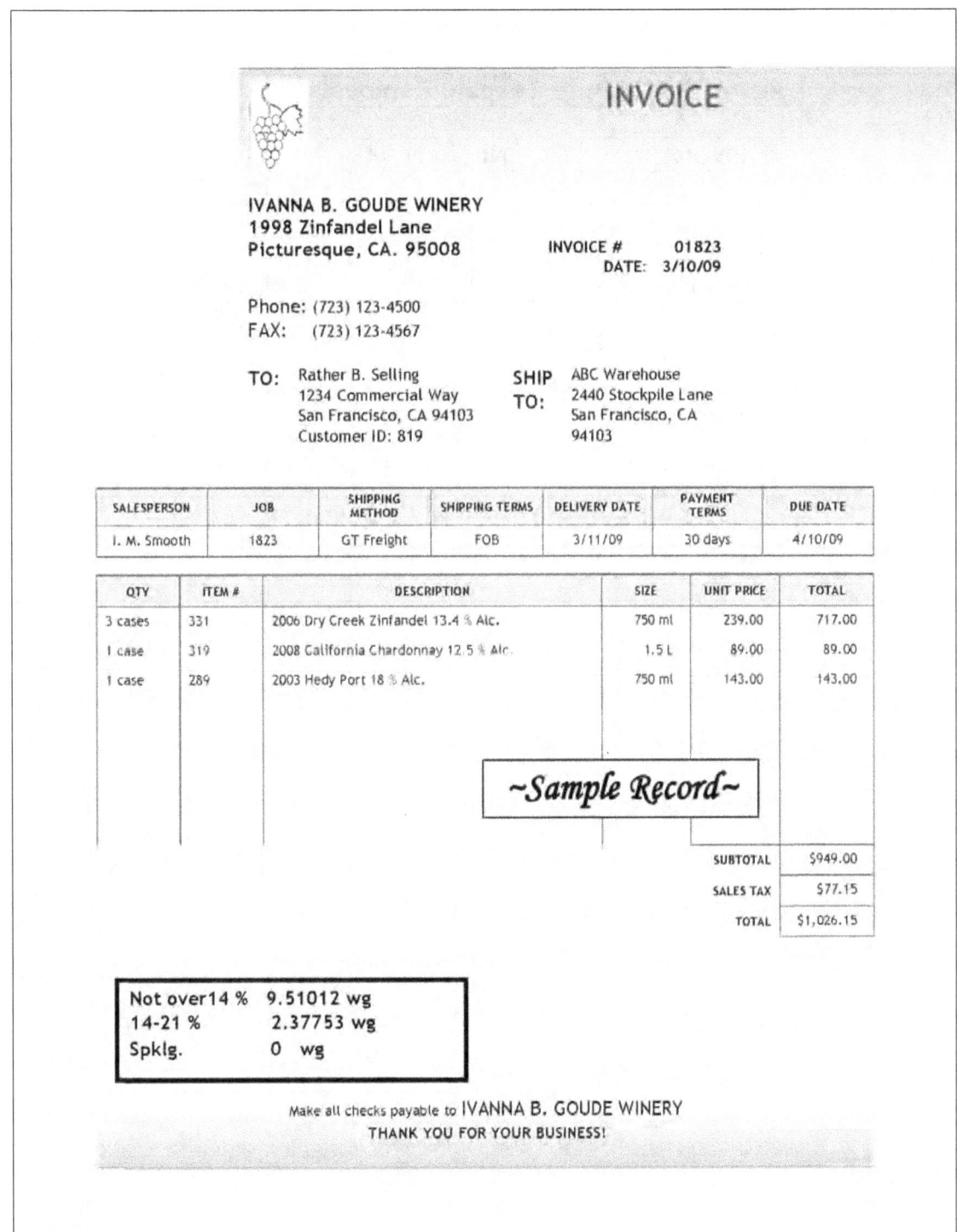

52

Here is an example of a daily summary that meets the requirements of 27 CFR 24.310, Taxpaid Removals from Bond Record, "The volume of wine removed taxpaid will be summarized daily by tax class in wine gallons to the nearest 10th gallon."

March 10, 2009	Taxpaid Removals	
Invoice #	Not over 14%	14-21%
1823 9.51012		2.37753
1824 0.39626		
1825 2.37753		
1826 9.51012		
1827		0.59438
Total 21.79403		2.97191
Daily Total	21.8 gal.	3.0 gal.

Taxpaid Wine Record
📖 27 CFR 24.311

When a bonded winery or bonded wine cellar has wine on the bonded premises that has *been taxpaid*, a separate record must be maintained which contains the information listed below. This information is not shown on the Report of Wine Premises Operations Form 5120.17.

Record of Receipt

☐ The name and address of the person or wine premises from whom received
☐ The registry number (if any) of the wine premises from which receive
☐ The date of receipt
☐ The kind of wine (class, type and, in the case of foreign wine, country of origin)
☐ Alcohol content or tax class of the wine
☐ The volume of wine received in liters and gallons

Record of Removals

☐ The name and address of the person to whom removed; however, on any individual sale of less than 80 liters, the name and address of the purchaser need not be recorded
☐ The date of removal
☐ The kind of wine (class, type and, in the case of foreign wine or a blend of US and foreign wine, country of origin)
☐ The volume of wine shipped in liters or gallons

Record of Cases or Containers Filled

☐ The date the cases or containers were filled
☐ The kind (class, type, and in the case of foreign wine or a blend of US and foreign wine, country of origin) of wine bottled or packed
☐ The number of the tank used to fill the bottles or other container
☐ The size of bottles or other containers and the number of cases or containers filled
☐ The serial number or date of fill marked on cases or containers filled
☐ The total volume of wine bottled or packed in liters or wine gallons

Taxpaid Wine Returned to Bond Record
27 CFR 24.312

A proprietor shall maintain a record of any *[unmerchantable*]* taxpaid wine returned to bond as follows:

(a) The kind, volume, and tax class of the wine;

(b) With regard to each tax class, the amount of tax previously paid or determined;

(c) The location of the wine premises at which the wine was bottled or packed and, if known, the identity of the bonded wine premises from which removed on determination of tax;

(d) The date the wine was returned to bond;

(e) The serial numbers or other identifying marks on the cases or containers in which the wine was received; and

(f) The final disposition of the wine.

[*Note: In accordance with a change made to Internal Revenue Code Law 26 U.S.C. 5044, wine returned to bond is not required to be "unmerchantable."]

UNTAXPAID REMOVALS

Wine excise tax does not have to be paid for certain removals from the bonded wine premises, if proper records are kept. These removals include the following:

- Testing on bonded premises or by an outside laboratory
  27 CFR 24.96 - .97

- Tasting on Bonded Premises
  27 CFR 24.97

- Family Use by sole proprietors, partnerships, and LLCs taxed as a partnership - up to 200 wine gallons per year, per household, or 100 gallons for a single person
  27 CFR 24.75

- Destruction – submit application and obtain permission from TTB prior to destruction
  27 CFR 24.294

- Breakage
  27 CFR 24.308

- Official Use of the Government – Samples taken by TTB
  27 CFR 24.293

- Transfer   in Bond
  27 CFR 24.309

- Export out of the United States
  27 CFR 24.292; 27 CFR Part 28

      Please refer to the regulations listed for more information.

Transfer in Bond Record

 27 CFR 24.309

When wine is transferred in bond, a record must be kept that contains the information listed below. The record may be a compilation of source documents OR a summary record.

☐ The date of shipment

☐ The name, address, and registry number of proprietor and consignee

☐ The kind of wine (class and type) and alcohol content or tax class

☐ The number of containers larger than 4 liters and cases

☐ The serial numbers of cases (if any) or containers larger than 4 liters, or other marks (bulk wine)

☐ The volume shipped in gallons or liters

☐ The serial number of any seal used

☐ Information necessary for compliance with 27 CFR 24.314 (Label Information Record) – the varietal, vintage, appellation of origin designation or any other information which may be stated on the label

☐ Information as to any added substance or cellar treatment for which a label designation may be required or where limitations are prescribed (includes sulfites) and kind and quantity of acid used

☐ For unlabeled bottled wine, the registry number of the bottler

A bill of lading used to ship bottled or bulk wine in bond from one bonded wine premises to another can contain all of the necessary information required by the Transfer in Bond Record 27 CFR 24.309. Here are examples of Transfer in Bond records for the in-bond shipment of bottled wine and bulk wine:

Bottled Wine Transferred in Bond

SHIPPING MEMORANDUM		By Truck	✓	Freight	

FROM: Ivana B Good Vyds.
ADDRESS: 1998 Zinfandel Lane
Picturesque, CA 950xx
REGISTRY NO.: BW-CA-9000

Date: May 30, 2009

Shipper's No. _____ 70037
Sales Order No. 09-042

CONSIGNEE: Consolidated Wine Cellar
ADDRESS: 200 West Main
Napa, CA 954xx
REGISTRY NO.: BW-CA-8000

CARRIER	CARRIER'S NO.
Heavy Hauling	
Route	Delivering Carrier
DEL TS-01-S-99	

TRANSFER IN BOND

CODE	QUANTITY	DESCRIPTION OF ARTICLES, SPECIAL MARKS & EXCEPTIONS	SIZE	WEIGHT
07RVPN	10 cs.	100% 2007 100% Pinot Noir 100% Russian River Valley	750 ml	360 lbs.
		14.1% alc by vol Contains Sulfites		
		~Sample Record~		

Total 1 Pieces: 0 cs.
Total Weight: 360 lbs

C.O.D Shipment
C.O.D. Amount _____
Fee _____
Total
Charges $ _____

Total Wine Gallons
23.78 gal. -14%

D. B. Cooperage
(Signature of Consignor)

Seal #'s:

Bulk Wine Transferred in Bond

| SHIPPING MEMORANDUM | | By Truck | ✓ | Freight | |

FROM:	Ivana B Good Vyds.	Date:	Shipper's No. _____ 70037
ADDRESS:	1998 Zinfandel Lane	May 30, 2009	
	Picturesque, CA 950xx		Sales Order No. _____ 09-042
REGISTRY NO.:	BW-CA-9000		

CONSIGNEE:	Consolidated Wine Cellar	CARRIER	CARRIER'S NO.
ADDRESS:	200 West Main	Heavy Hauling	
	Napa, CA 954xx	Route	Delivering Carrier
REGISTRY NO.:	BW-CA-8000	DEL TS-01-S-99	

TRANSFER IN BOND

CODE	QUANTITY	DESCRIPTION OF ARTICLES, SPECIAL MARKS & EXCEPTIONS	SIZE	WEIGHT
07RVPN	1	100% 2007 100% Pinot Noir	3060	24500
		100% Russian River Valley	gals.	lbs.
		14.1% alc by vol		
		Contains Sulfites		
		~Sample Record~		

Total 1 Pieces

Total Weight 24500 lbs.

C.O.D Shipment	
C.O.D. Amount	_____
Fee	_____
Total	
Charges $	_____

Total Wine Gallons
3060 gal. -14%

D. B. Cooperage
(Signature of Consignor)

Seal #'s:

Exporting Wine Out of the United States
27 CFR 24.292; 27 CFR Part 28

1) Wine may be exported out of the United States taxpaid or untaxpaid.

📕   See 27 CFR Part 28 – Exportation of Alcohol

🖱   http://www.ttb.gov/other/regulations.shtml

Untaxpaid: Submit Form 5100.11 and proof of export to TTB in accordance with 27 CFR Part 28, subpart F.   Volume exported is shown on Report of Wine Premises Operations Form 5120.17.

Taxpaid: Submit Forms 5120.24, 5120.20 and proof of export to TTB for tax refund or credit in accordance with 27 CFR Part 28, subpart K. Volume exported is shown on Report of Wine Premises Operations Form 5120.17 as a taxable removal, not as an export.

2) Industry Circular 2004-3 "Alcohol and Tobacco Export Documentation Procedures"

🖱    http://www.ttb.gov/wine/wine_ic.shtml

   ✓ Lists the documentation that is acceptable proof for each type of export.

   ✓ Gives the guidelines for requesting permission to maintain export documentation at your place of business

   ✓ See further information in "IC 2004-3 FAQs"

3) International Trade Resources - a thorough listing of international trade resources for wine, beer and distilled spirits, including requirements for licensing, labeling, and taxation considerations.

🖱   http://www.ttb.gov/itd/index.shtml

4) Industry Circulars regarding VI-1 Forms for export to the European Union, Qualification as a Certified Laboratory, Export to Japan:

Industry Circular	Title	Date
2007-2	Certification and Analysis of U.S. Wine for Exportation to the EC	6/21/2007
1988-1	Certification and Analysis of U.S. Wine for Export to the EEC	8/18/1988
1986-6	Certification and Analysis of U.S. Wine for Export to the EEC	3/17/1986
1986-3	Certification of Chemists, Enologists and Laboratories for the Analysis of Wine for Export	1/24/1986
1986-2	Certification and Analysis of U.S. Wine for Export to the EEC	1/24/1986

5) TTB Certified Chemists for analysis of wine and spirits for export:

http://www.ttb.gov/ssd/chemist_certification.shtml

6) Current Members of the European Union

The European Union (EU), also referred to as the European Community (EC), requires that a document known as the "VI-1" (Document for the Importation of Wine, Grape Juice or Must into the European Community) be used when you export wines to the EU. If you export wine to any of the countries listed below, you must complete the VI-1 form or the new simplified certificate.

Austria	Germany	Netherlands
Belgium	Greece	Poland
Bulgaria	Hungary	Portugal
Cyprus	Ireland	Romania
Czech Republic	Italy	Slovakia
Denmark	Latvia	Slovenia
Estonia	Lithuania	Spain
Finland	Luxembourg	Sweden
France	Malta	United Kingdom

When wine is exported out of the United States **without payment of tax**, Form 5100.11 with proof of export must be submitted to TTB. Industry Circular 2004-3 gives the guidelines for requesting permission to maintain these documents at the wine premises. See 27 CFR 28.121-133.

OMB No. 1513-0037 (01/31/2012)

DEPARTMENT OF THE TREASURY
ALCOHOL AND TOBACCO TAX AND TRADE BUREAU (TTB)
WITHDRAWAL OF SPIRITS, SPECIALLY DENATURED SPIRITS, OR WINES FOR EXPORTATION
Please read Instructions after Page 2 before completing this form.

1. SERIAL NO. (Begin with "1" each Jan. 1)

PART I - APPLICATION OR NOTICE

2. APPLICATION IS MADE TO
- [ ] WITHDRAW SPIRITS OR WINES WITHOUT PAYMENT OF TAX

3. NOTICE GIVEN OF
- [ ] WITHDRAWAL OF SPECIALLY DENATURED SPIRITS FREE OF TAX
- [ ] WITHDRAWAL OF SPIRITS OR WINES WITHOUT PAYMENT OF TAX

4. WITHDRAWAL FROM
- [ ] BWC. _____
- [ ] DSP. _____

OPERATED BY

5. ADDRESS OF DIRECTOR, NATIONAL REVENUE CENTER ALCOHOL AND TOBACCO TAX AND TRADE BUREAU
550 MAIN ST, STE 8002
CINCINNATI, OH 45202-5215

6. PURPOSE OF WITHDRAWAL (Make Applicable Entries)
- [ ] SHIPMENT FOR EXPORT TO ARMED FORCES OF THE U.S.
- [ ] FOR EXPORTATION TO (Name the foreign port and country)

TRANSFER TO (Number or name and location)
- [ ] CMBW [ ] FTZ [ ] CBW

USE AS SUPPLIES ON VESSELS [ ] 1/ AIRCRAFT [ ] 1/

7. CONSIGNED TO OR IN CARE OF (Make applicable entries)
- [ ] DIRECTOR OF CUSTOMS AT PORT OF (Specify)
- [ ] TRANSPORTATION OFFICER (Name) (Location)
- [ ] CUSTOMS OFFICER/WAREHOUSE PROPRIETOR OF [ ] CMBW [ ] FTZ [ ] CBW (Location)

8. NAME OF DOMESTIC CARRIER

9. NAME OF EXPORT CARRIER

10. DESCRIPTION OF SPIRITS OR DENATURED SPIRITS AND CONTAINERS (Columns a, d, e, and f only are required for denatured spirits)

KIND 2/ (a)	PRODUCED BY [ ] FILLED BY [ ] NAME (b)	DSP NO. (c)	CONTAINERS		PG 3/ [ ] WG (f)
			NO. AND TYPE (d)	IDENTIFICATION (e)	

11. DESCRIPTION OF WINES AND CONTAINERS

KIND (a)	PERCENT ALCOHOL (b)	CONTAINERS		BOTTLES PER CASE (e)	SIZE OF BOTTLES (f)	WINE GALLONS (g)	TAX LIABILITY (h)
		NO. AND TYPE (c)	SERIAL NUMBER 4/ (d)				

Under the penalties of perjury, I declare that the spirits, denatured spirits, or wines described above are truly intended to (or have been) withdrawn for the purpose indicated, in the manner prescribed in regulations, and will not be (have not been) shipped for the purpose of evading or delaying payment of any revenue tax thereon.

12. DATE	13. PRINCIPAL 5/	13a. SIGNATURE	13b. TITLE

FOR TTB USE ONLY PART II - APPROVAL OF APPLICATION

Application is approved with respect to the required bond	14. DATE	15. SIGNATURE AND TITLE OF APPROVING OFFICER

1/ State whether (a) vessel or aircraft operated by the United States, (b) vessel or aircraft engaged in foreign trade, or in trade between the United States and any of its possessions, or between Hawaii or Alaska and any other part of the United States; (c) vessel of the United States engaged in trade between Atlantic and Pacific ports of the United States; (d) vessel of war of any foreign nation; or (e) vessel employed in: (1) the fisheries; or (2) the whaling business. Show name of vessel, country of registry, and ports of call, or, if a whaling vessel, location of operations. If aircraft, show also name of airline and country of registry of aircraft.
2/ Also enter formula number for special denatured spirits.
3/ Enter quantity of spirits in proof gallons or quantity of denatured spirits in wine gallons and check applicable box.
4/ In items 11(d) and 22 show filling date when use of that date is authorized instead of serial numbers on cases. Item 11(d) need not be completed when prior approval of application is required.
5/ Show principal on bond under which withdrawal is made.

TTB F 5100.11 (10/2009)   Page 1 of 2

When **taxpaid wine is exported** out of the United States, the exporter may submit a claim for drawback of the excise tax previous paid by submitting Forms 5120.24, 5120.20 and proof of export to TTB.   See 27 CFR 28.211-220a.

OMB No. 1513-0016 (01/31/2010)

DEPARTMENT OF THE TREASURY
ALCOHOL AND TOBACCO TAX AND TRADE BUREAU
DRAWBACK ON WINES EXPORTED
(See instructions below)

1. SERIAL NUMBER (begin with "1" each Jan 1)

(NRC USE ONLY)

PART I - NOTICE

2. TO DIRECTOR, NRC — Director, National Revenue Center / Alcohol and Tobacco Tax and Trade Bureau, 550 Main St., Ste 8002, Cincinnati, OH 45202-5215

The undersigned gives notice of the shipment of wines manufactured, bottled, or packaged in the United States on which drawback of the Internal Revenue tax paid or determined is claimed.

CLAIM NUMBER

3. EXPORTER - NAME AND ADDRESS (Number, Street, City, State, Zip Code)

4. NUMBER

DATE RECEIVED

TTB F 5620.5

FILED WITH CLAIM NO.

5. EMPLOYER IDENTIFICATION NUMBER

6. PURPOSE OF SHIPMENT (Make applicable entries)

☐ SHIPMENT FOR EXPORT TO ARMED FORCES OF THE U.S. ☐ TRANSFER TO FOREIGN TRADE ZONE (Number) (Location)

AMOUNT CLAIMED $

EXPORTATION TO (Name of foreign port and country)

AMOUNT REJECTED $

USE AS SUPPLIES ON ☐ A VESSEL? ☐ AIRCRAFT?

AMOUNT APPROVED $

CLAIMS CLERK

7. CONSIGNED TO OR IN CARE OF (Make applicable entries)

PORT DIRECTOR OF CUSTOMS AT PORT OF

TRANSPORTATION OFFICER (Name) (Location)

8. NAME OF DOMESTIC CARRIER

CUSTOMS OFFICER IN CHARGE OF FOREIGN TRADE ZONE (Number) (Location)

9. NAME OF EXPORT CARRIER

10. DESCRIPTION OF WINE SHIPPED

KIND OF WINE (a)	NUMBER OF PACKAGES (b)	CASES			SERIAL NUMBERS OF CONTAINERS OR CASES⁴ (f)	ALCOL CONTENT (g)	TOTAL WINE GALLONS (h)	DRAWBACK RATE PER WINE GALLON (i)
		NUMBER (c)	BOTTLES in case (d)	size (e)				

PART II - CLAIM

The wines described in Part I have been removed for the purpose stated, and are not to be brought back or relanded within the limits of the United States. The kind, quantity, and description of the wines stated in Part I is correct, and I am justly entitled to drawback of the tax in the amount claimed herein. Internal Revenue tax equal to such amount has been paid or determined as provided by law and regulations. No other claim for allowance of drawback has been made under 26 U.S.C. 5062(b), or Section 309 of the Tariff Act of 1930, as amended, on these wines or any part thereof. Under penalties of perjury, I declare that I have examined Part I hereof, and this claim, and to the best of my knowledge and belief the statements herein and in Part I, are true, correct, and complete.

11. AMOUNT CLAIMED $

12. I REQUEST DRAWBACK ALLOWED TO BE PAID BY ☐ CHECK ☐ CREDIT

13. DATE

14. EXPORTER

14a. BY (Signature and Title)

¹Insert, as applicable, plant number of distilled spirits plant, registry number of bonded wine cellar or taxpaid wine bottling house, or number of the wholesale liquor dealers permit issued under the Federal Alcohol Administration Act
²Complete only for consolidated claims; show serial number of last claim tabulated
³State whether a (a) vessel or aircraft operated by the United States; (b) vessel or aircraft engaged in foreign trade, or in trade between the United States and any of its possessions, or between Hawaii or Alaska and any other part of the United States;

(c) vessel of the United States engaged in trade between Atlantic and Pacific ports of the United States; (d) vessel employed in country of registry, and ports of call, or if a whaling vessel, location of operations. If aircraft, show also name of airline and country of registry of aircraft.
⁴Show filing date when use of such date has been authorized in lieu of serial numbers on cases.

TTB F 5120.24 (4/2007)

Page 1 of 2

Form 5120.20, Certificate of Tax Determination – Wine, must accompany all Forms 5120.24, Drawback on Wines Exported:

OMB No. 1513-0029 (11/30/2009)

DEPARTMENT OF THE TREASURY
ALCOHOL AND TOBACCO TAX AND TRADE BUREAU (TTB)
CERTIFICATE OF TAX DETERMINATION - WINE
(See Paperwork Reduction Act Notice Below)

FILED IN SUPPORT OF
TTB FORM 5120.24
SERIAL NO.

PART I - STATEMENT OF EXPORTER

I am the exporter of wines described below, and intend to file claim for drawback of tax thereon.

KINDS OF WINES (a)	A C L O C N O T H E O N L T (b)	NO. OF PACK-AGES (c)	NUMBER OF CASES (d)	PER CS. (e)	SIZE (f)	TRADE OR BRAND NAME (g)	SERIAL NUMBERS (Show filing date when use of such date has been authorized in lieu of serial numbers on cases) (h)	WINE GALLONS (i)

1. DATE

2. EXPORTER (Name and Address)

3. BY (Signature and Title)

PART II - REQUEST OF EXPORTER FOR CERTIFICATE

4a. TO: (Name and Address)

4b. My records indicate that the above described wines were:

☐ Withdrawn by you on determination of tax

☐ Bottled or packaged by you after determination of tax

Please execute the certificate (Part III) on all copies of this form, and return the original and one copy to me at the address shown above.

PART III - CERTIFICATE

5. Under penalties of perjury, I certify that the wines described above were manufactured or produced in the United States and were:

☐ Bottled or packaged while in bond, and were then withdrawn from bond by me on determination of tax.

☐ Withdrawn from bond by me on determination of tax and were then bottled or packaged by me.

☐ Bottled or packaged by me after they were received in taxpaid status from:

(NAME, ADDRESS, AND PLANT OR PERMIT NUMBER)

This certificate is executed with the knowledge that it will be used in support of a claim against the United States for drawback of tax.

6. DATE

7. DEPONENT (Name and Address)

8. BY (Signature and Title)

9. PLANT OR PERMIT NO.

INSTRUCTIONS

1. A certificate of tax determination must be executed on this form to support a claim filed by an exporter for drawback of tax on wines exported from the United States, laden for use as supplies on certain vessels or aircraft, transferred to a foreign-trade zone, or transferred for export to Armed Forces of the United States. Prepare an original and two copies of the form (original and one if the exporter and the person executing Part III of the form are the same).

2. Part III of the form is for certifying that the wines were produced or manufactured in the United States and were properly tax paid on withdrawal from bond. This part may

be executed only (a) by the person who withdrew the wine from bond on determination of tax, or (b) if the wine was bottled or packaged after tax determination, by the person who bottled or packaged it.

3. The exporter is responsible for securing a properly executed certificate. The original of the form must be submitted to the Director, National Revenue Center, 550 Main St, Ste 8002, Cincinnati, OH 45202-5215. A copy of the form must be retained by the exporter and by the person who executes Part III for 3 years.

TTB F 5120.20 (8/2009)

Federal Excise Tax Rates per Gallon
📖 26 U.S.C. 5041(b)

There are six tax rates given in the Internal Revenue Code for wine products:

Not over 14% alcohol	$1.07*
Over 14% but not over 21% alcohol	$1.57*
Over 21% but not over 24% alcohol	$3.15*
Artificially Carbonated Wine	$3.30*
Sparkling Wine $3.40	
Hard Cider** $	.226*

* A tax credit which reduces these rates by as much as $ .90 per gallon is available to certain producers for a portion of the company's taxable removals each calendar year.

** Hard Cider is a still (not effervescent) apple wine product that contains less than 7% alcohol by volume. Credit of as much as $ .056 per gallon is available to certain producers of hard cider. See 27 CFR 24.10.

Federal Excise Tax Periods and Due Dates
27 CFR 24.271 and 27 CFR 24.273

Tax Periods		Tax Return Due Dates*
Semi-Monthly 1	st -15th day of each month and the 16th day through the last day of each month	Not later than the 14th day after the last day of the return period.
September	Special rules apply	See Tax Return Calendar.
Quarterly	Calendar Quarters	Not later than the 14th day after the last day of the quarter.
Annual	Calendar Year	Not later than the 30th day after the last day of the calendar year.
*Exception: If the due date falls on a Saturday, Sunday, or legal holiday, the return and remittance is due on the immediately preceding day which is not a Saturday, Sunday or legal holiday, except as noted in the special filing provisions for the month of September (see 27 CFR 24.271(c)(3)).		

Quarterly Excise Tax Payments
📖 27 CFR 24.271

Some wine premises may submit Excise Tax Returns and tax payment quarterly, if the following conditions are met:

1. The Excise Taxes totaled not more than $50,000 the previous calendar year, and

2. The Excise Taxes will total not more than $50,000 the current calendar year, and

3. Sufficient deferral coverage is provided.

If mailed, the tax return and tax must be postmarked not later than the 14th day after the close of the calendar quarter. If filed using the Pay.Gov program, ACH payment must be completed no later than 4:00 PM Eastern Time one business day prior to the due date.

If the $50,000 limit is exceeded during the calendar year, the taxes must be paid immediately. Twice-monthly filing must resume for the rest of the calendar year, as well as during the following calendar year.

Annual Excise Tax Payments
📖 27 CFR 24.273

Some wine premises may submit one Excise Tax Return and tax payment annually, if the following conditions are met:

1. If the Excise Taxes totaled less than $1,000 the previous calendar year, and

2. The Excise Taxes will total less than $1,000 the current calendar year, and

3. Sufficient deferral coverage is provided, and additional deferral coverage has not been given.

If mailed, the tax return and tax must be postmarked not later than the 30th day after the close of the calendar year. If filed using the Pay.Gov program, ACH payment must be completed no later than 4:00 PM Eastern Time one business day prior to the due date.

If the $1,000 limit is reached during the calendar year, the taxes must be paid immediately. Twice-monthly or quarterly (if eligible) filing must resume for the rest of the calendar year, as well as during the following calendar year.

Alcohol & Tobacco Due Dates for Semi-Monthly Tax Returns
for Revenue Producing Plants ~ Calendar Year 2010

Serial Number	Return Period	Due Date
1	January 1-15, 2010	January 29, 2010
2	January 16-31	February 12
3	February 1-15	March 1
4	February 16-28	March 12
5	March 1-15	March 29
6	March 16-31	April 14
7	April 1-15	April 29
8	April 16-30	May 14
9	May 1-15	May 28
10	May 16-31	June 14
11	June 1-15	June 29
12	June 16-30	July 14
13	July 1-15	July 29
14	July 16-31	August 13
15	August 1-15	August 27
16	August 16-31	September 14
17	September 1-15	September 29
18	September 16-25	September 28 Non-EFT
18	September 16-26	September 29 EFT
19	September 26-30	October 14 Non-EFT
19	September 27-30	October 14 EFT
20	October 1-15	October 29
21	October 16-31	November 12
22	November 1-15	November 29
23	November 16-30	December 14
24	December 1-15	December 29
25	December 16-31	January 14, 2011

The above list takes into account all federal holidays. In the event that the due date, as indicated in this schedule, falls on a statewide legal holiday in the state where the return is required to be filed, the due date is the immediately preceding date which is not a Saturday, Sunday or legal holiday for Non-EFT payers.

Statewide legal holidays would not advance the due date of EFT tax returns and payments, as long as the Federal Reserve Bank of New York City remains open and accepts electronic fund transfer payments.

For Pay.gov payments: ACH payments must be completed no later than 4:00 PM Eastern Time one business day prior to the due date.

Alcohol & Tobacco Due Dates for Quarterly Tax Returns
for Revenue Producing Plants ~ Calendar Year 2010

Serial Number	Return Period	Due Date
1	January 1 – March 31, 2010	April 14, 2010
2	April 1 – June 30, 2010	July 14, 2010
3	July 1 – September 30, 2010	October 14, 2010
4	October 1 – December 31, 2010	January 14, 2011

Public Law 109-59 amended 26 USC 5061 to allow proprietors of distilled spirits plants, bonded wineries, bonded wine cellars and breweries who were liable for not more than $50,000 distilled spirits, wine or beer excise tax in the previous calendar year, and who reasonably expect to be liable for not more than $50,000 in such taxes in the current year to file tax returns on a quarterly basis.

NOTE: Be sure that bond coverage is sufficient before you elect to file returns on a quarterly basis. Refer to guidance posted on our web site at www.ttb.gov concerning how to qualify for quarterly filing or call us at 1-877-882-3277.

The above list takes into account all federal holidays. In the event that the due date, as indicated in this schedule, falls on a statewide legal holiday in the state where the return is required to be filed, the due date is the immediately preceding date which is not a Saturday, Sunday or legal holiday for Non-EFT payers.

Statewide legal holidays would not advance the due date of EFT tax returns and payments, as long as the Federal Reserve Bank of New York City remains open and accepts electronic fund transfer payments.

For Pay.gov payments: ACH payments must be completed no later than 4:00 PM Eastern Time one business day prior to the due date.

Safe Harbor Rule for September Taxes
📖 27 CFR 24.271(c)(2)

The wine excise tax due for the second tax period in September may be paid using the Safe Harbor Rule, as follows:

	Tax Period	Amount Due	Due Date
EFT taxpayers	Sept. 1-15	100% of taxes due for Sept. 1-15	September 29
Sept.	16-26	73.3% of taxes incurred Sept. 1-15	September 29
Sept.	27-30	100% of taxes due for Sept. 27-30 + rest of taxes due for Sept. 16-26	October 14
Non-EFT taxpayers	Sept. 1-15	100% of taxes due for Sept. 1-15	September 29
Sept.	16-25	66.7% of taxes incurred Sept. 1-15	September 28
Sept.	26-30	100% of taxes due for Sept. 26-30 + rest of taxes due for Sept. 16-26	October 14

Payment by Electronic Fund Transfer
📖 27 CFR 24.272

Some companies are required to pay their wine excise taxes by electronic fund transfer (EFT) rather than by check or other forms of payment.

- EFT is required if the gross amount of wine excise tax liability was $5 million or more during the previous calendar year.

- The gross liability includes all domestic taxable removals and the tax on imported wine, before consideration of refunds, credits or drawback.

- The gross liability of all members of a controlled group are considered, and all members of a controlled group required to EFT must make tax payments by EFT.

See Procedure 91-1, "TTB Procedure for Payment of Tax by Electronic Fund Transfer," for detailed guidance on filing taxes by EFT.

🖱 http://www.ttb.gov/procedures/91-1.shtml

Penalties and Interest

When a company fails to file a required tax return, make timely tax payment or deposits, or willfully neglects to pay taxes, the Government may impose certain financial penalties. If tax is underpaid due to fraud, the taxpayer may be subject to a civil fraud penalty. In certain cases, the taxpayer may be subject to criminal prosecution.

This is a brief overview of the most common types of penalties imposed. It is not intended to be inclusive of all penalties assessable by the Federal Government. This information is given to help reduce the likelihood of incurring such liabilities.

Failure to File (FF) Penalty is equal to 5% of the tax not paid by the due date for each month or part of a month that the return is late. This penalty cannot be more than 25% of the tax. If taxes are paid by Electronic Fund Transfer, the taxpayer is responsible for the timely filing of the tax return.

Failure to Pay (FP) Penalty is equal to 1/2 of 1% of the unpaid taxes for each month or part of a month after the due date that the tax is not paid. This penalty cannot be more than 25% of the unpaid tax. If a penalty for FF and a penalty for FP both apply for the same month, the amount of the penalty for failure to file for that month is reduced by the amount of the penalty for failure to pay tax shown on a return.

Failure to Deposit (FTD) Penalty is charged for failure to deposit correctly. The three components of a correct deposit are that it is made timely, in the correct amount, and in the correct manner. Failure to comply with any of these components may invoke the FTD Penalty. Deposits are due on or before the deposit due date. The penalty rate ranges from 2% to 15% of the underpayment depending on the number of days a deposit is late.

Interest, compounded daily, is charged on any unpaid tax from the due date of the return until the date of payment.

For more information on determining the rate of interest, as well as a table of interest rates, please see Internal Revenue Service Revenue Ruling 2008-54.

http://www.irs.gov/pub/irs-drop/rr-08-54.pdf

This is an example of a properly completed <u>semi-monthly</u> Excise Tax Return:

Small Domestic Producer Credit
26 U.S.C. 5041(c); 27 CFR 24.278-279

Who is allowed to use the Small Domestic Producer Credit?
Domestic producers of not more than 250,000 wine gallons during a calendar year are allowed up to 90 cents per gallon on the 1st 100,000 wine gallons of wine (other than sparkling wines) which are removed during the same year for consumption or sale. The credit on hard cider is up to 5.6 cents per gallon, rather than 90 cents per gallon.

What figures are used to determine how much wine was produced?
The amount of wine produced for small domestic producer credit purposes is the total of the amount produced by fermentation plus any volume increases due to wine produced by amelioration, wine spirits addition, sweetening, production of a formula wine, sparkling wine, and wine produced by the same company outside the United States.

When does a wine taxpayer use less than 90 cents per gallon credit? If the amount of wine produced during the year exceeds 150,000 wine gallons, the credit is reduced by 1% for every 1,000 wine gallons of wine produced in excess of 150,000 wine gallons.

How is the credit used by Controlled Groups? The production and taxable removal of wine by all members of a controlled group are added together when determining if the Small Domestic Producer Credit may be used. The credit may be taken on the first 100,000 gallons taxably removed by all members of the controlled group.

Can the credit be transferred to another taxpayer? The credit may be transferred to another taxpayer as long as the transferring (sending) winery would be eligible to use the credit if it paid the tax itself, produced the wine, holds title to the wine, and provides the taxpayer with sufficient information to pay the tax correctly using the credit.

Small Domestic Producer Credit Production Levels
📖 26 U.S.C. 5041(c) and 27 CFR 24.278-.279

The amount of small domestic producer credit a company may use depends upon the amount of wine produced each calendar year:

If Production is:	Credit	Available Per Year is:
150,000 gallons or less	=	$ .90 per gallon on first 100,000 gallons taxably removed per calendar year
(Exception:		transferred credit)
Over 150,000 to 250,000	=	$ .89 - $ .01 per gallon on first 100,000 gallons taxably removed per calendar year. See chart on next page for the effective tax rates.
(Exception:		transferred credit)
More than 250,000 gallons	=	None available
(Exception:		transferred credit)
No Production	=	None available
(Exception:		transferred credit)

- The production and removals of all members of a controlled group are added together to determine how much wine was produced and removed by the company as a whole each calendar year.

- All removals beyond 100,000 gallons each year calendar year must be tax paid at the full tax rate.

- Credit may not be used on the taxable removal of Sparkling Wine.

If more than 150,000 gallons, but not more than 250,000 gallons, are produced, the credit is reduced by 1% for every 1,000 gallons produced:

Production Level		Credit Amount		Effective Tax on 1st 100,000 Gallons				
From	To	%	$	<=14%	14-21%	21-24%	Art Carb	Hard Cider
Less than	150,999.9	100%	0.900	0.17	0.67	2.25	2.40	0.17
151,000	151,999.9	99%	0.891	0.179	0.679	2.259	2.409	0.171
152,000	152,999.9	98%	0.882	0.188	0.688	2.268	2.418	0.171
153,000	153,999.9	97%	0.873	0.197	0.697	2.277	2.427	0.172
154,000	154,999.9	96%	0.864	0.206	0.706	2.286	2.436	0.172
155,000	155,999.9	95%	0.855	0.215	0.715	2.295	2.445	0.173
156,000	156,999.9	94%	0.846	0.224	0.724	2.304	2.454	0.173
157,000	157,999.9	93%	0.837	0.233	0.733	2.313	2.463	0.174
158,000	158,999.9	92%	0.828	0.242	0.742	2.322	2.472	0.174
159,000	159,999.9	91%	0.819	0.251	0.751	2.331	2.481	0.175
160,000	160,999.9	90%	0.810	0.260	0.760	2.340	2.490	0.176
161,000	161,999.9	89%	0.801	0.269	0.769	2.349	2.499	0.176
162,000	162,999.9	88%	0.792	0.278	0.778	2.358	2.508	0.177
163,000	163,999.9	87%	0.783	0.287	0.787	2.367	2.517	0.177
164,000	164,999.9	86%	0.774	0.296	0.796	2.376	2.526	0.178
165,000	165,999.9	85%	0.765	0.305	0.805	2.385	2.535	0.178
166,000	166,999.9	84%	0.756	0.314	0.814	2.394	2.544	0.179
167,000	167,999.9	83%	0.747	0.323	0.823	2.403	2.553	0.183
168,000	168,999.9	82%	0.738	0.332	0.832	2.412	2.562	0.180
169,000	169,999.9	81%	0.729	0.341	0.841	2.421	2.571	0.181
170,000	170,999.9	80%	0.720	0.350	0.850	2.430	2.580	0.181
171,000	171,999.9	79%	0.711	0.359	0.859	2.439	2.589	0.182
172,000	172,999.9	78%	0.702	0.368	0.868	2.448	2.598	0.182
173,000	173,999.9	77%	0.693	0.377	0.877	2.457	2.607	0.183
174,000	174,999.9	76%	0.684	0.386	0.886	2.466	2.616	0.183
175,000	175,999.9	75%	0.675	0.395	0.895	2.475	2.625	0.184
176,000	176,999.9	74%	0.666	0.404	0.904	2.484	2.634	0.185
177,000	177,999.9	73%	0.657	0.413	0.913	2.493	2.643	0.185
178,000	178,999.9	72%	0.648	0.422	0.922	2.502	2.652	0.186
179,000	179,999.9	71%	0.639	0.431	0.931	2.511	2.661	0.186
180,000	180,999.9	70%	0.630	0.440	0.940	2.520	2.670	0.187
181,000	181,999.9	69%	0.621	0.449	0.949	2.529	2.679	0.187
182,000	182,999.9	68%	0.612	0.458	0.958	2.538	2.688	0.188
183,000	183,999.9	67%	0.603	0.467	0.967	2.547	2.697	0.188
184,000	184,999.9	66%	0.594	0.476	0.976	2.556	2.706	0.189
185,000	185,999.9	65%	0.585	0.485	0.985	2.565	2.715	0.190
186,000	186,999.9	64%	0.576	0.494	0.994	2.574	2.724	0.190
187,000	187,999.9	63%	0.567	0.503	1.003	2.583	2.733	0.191
188,000	188,999.9	62%	0.558	0.512	1.012	2.592	2.742	0.191
189,000	189,999.9	61%	0.549	0.521	1.021	2.601	2.751	0.192
190,000	190,999.9	60%	0.540	0.530	1.030	2.610	2.760	0.192
191,000	191,999.9	59%	0.531	0.539	1.039	2.619	2.769	0.193
192,000	192,999.9	58%	0.522	0.548	1.048	2.628	2.778	0.194
193,000	193,999.9	57%	0.513	0.557	1.057	2.637	2.787	0.194
194,000	194,999.9	56%	0.504	0.566	1.066	2.646	2.796	0.195
195,000	195,999.9	55%	0.495	0.575	1.075	2.655	2.805	0.195
196,000	196,999.9	54%	0.486	0.584	1.084	2.664	2.814	0.196
197,000	197,999.9	53%	0.477	0.593	1.093	2.673	2.823	0.196
198,000	198,999.9	52%	0.468	0.602	1.102	2.682	2.832	0.197
199,000	199,999.9	51%	0.459	0.611	1.111	2.691	2.841	0.197

Production Level		Credit Amount		Effective Tax on 1st 100,000 Gallons				
From	To	%	$	<=14%	14-21%	21-24%	Art Carb	Hard Cider
200,000	200,999.9	50%	0.450	0.620	1.120	2.700	2.850	0.198
201,000	201,999.9	49%	0.441	0.629	1.129	2.709	2.859	0.199
202,000	202,999.9	48%	0.432	0.638	1.138	2.718	2.868	0.199
203,000	203,999.9	47%	0.423	0.647	1.147	2.727	2.877	0.200
204,000	204,999.9	46%	0.414	0.656	1.156	2.736	2.886	0.200
205,000	205,999.9	45%	0.405	0.665	1.165	2.745	2.895	0.201
206,000	206,999.9	44%	0.396	0.674	1.174	2.754	2.904	0.201
207,000	207,999.9	43%	0.387	0.683	1.183	2.763	2.913	0.202
208,000	208,999.9	42%	0.378	0.692	1.192	2.772	2.922	0.202
209,000	209,999.9	41%	0.369	0.701	1.201	2.781	2.931	0.203
210,000	210,999.9	40%	0.360	0.710	1.210	2.790	2.940	0.204
211,000	211,999.9	39%	0.351	0.719	1.219	2.799	2.949	0.204
212,000	212,999.9	38%	0.342	0.728	1.228	2.808	2.958	0.205
213,000	213,999.9	37%	0.333	0.737	1.237	2.817	2.967	0.205
214,000	214,999.9	36%	0.324	0.746	1.246	2.826	2.976	0.206
215,000	215,999.9	35%	0.315	0.755	1.255	2.835	2.985	0.206
216,000	216,999.9	34%	0.306	0.764	1.264	2.844	2.994	0.207
217,000	217,999.9	33%	0.297	0.773	1.273	2.853	3.003	0.208
218,000	218,999.9	32%	0.288	0.782	1.282	2.862	3.012	0.208
219,000	219,999.9	31%	0.279	0.791	1.291	2.871	3.021	0.209
220,000	220,999.9	30%	0.270	0.800	1.300	2.880	3.030	0.209
221,000	221,999.9	29%	0.261	0.809	1.309	2.889	3.039	0.210
222,000	222,999.9	28%	0.252	0.818	1.318	2.898	3.048	0.210
223,000	223,999.9	27%	0.243	0.827	1.327	2.907	3.057	0.211
224,000	224,999.9	26%	0.234	0.836	1.336	2.916	3.066	0.211
225,000	225,999.9	25%	0.225	0.845	1.345	2.925	3.075	0.212
226,000	226,999.9	24%	0.216	0.854	1.354	2.934	3.084	0.213
227,000	227,999.9	23%	0.207	0.863	1.363	2.943	3.093	0.213
228,000	228,999.9	22%	0.198	0.872	1.372	2.952	3.102	0.214
229,000	229,999.9	21%	0.189	0.881	1.381	2.961	3.111	0.214
230,000	230,999.9	20%	0.180	0.890	1.390	2.970	3.120	0.215
231,000	231,999.9	19%	0.171	0.899	1.399	2.979	3.129	0.215
232,000	232,999.9	18%	0.162	0.908	1.408	2.988	3.138	0.216
233,000	233,999.9	17%	0.153	0.917	1.417	2.997	3.147	0.216
234,000	234,999.9	16%	0.144	0.926	1.426	3.006	3.156	0.217
235,000	235,999.9	15%	0.135	0.935	1.435	3.015	3.165	0.218
236,000	236,999.9	14%	0.126	0.944	1.444	3.024	3.174	0.218
237,000	237,999.9	13%	0.117	0.953	1.453	3.033	3.183	0.219
238,000	238,999.9	12%	0.108	0.962	1.462	3.042	3.192	0.219
239,000	239,999.9	11%	0.099	0.971	1.471	3.051	3.201	0.220
240,000	240,999.9	10%	0.090	0.980	1.480	3.060	3.210	0.220
241,000	241,999.9	9%	0.081	0.989	1.489	3.069	3.219	0.221
242,000	242,999.9	8%	0.072	0.998	1.498	3.078	3.228	0.222
243,000	243,999.9	7%	0.063	1.007	1.507	3.087	3.237	0.222
244,000	244,999.9	6%	0.054	1.016	1.516	3.096	3.246	0.223
245,000	245,999.9	5%	0.045	1.025	1.525	3.105	3.255	0.223
246,000	246,999.9	4%	0.036	1.034	1.534	3.114	3.264	0.224
247,000	247,999.9	3%	0.027	1.043	1.543	3.123	3.273	0.224
248,000	248,999.9	2%	0.018	1.052	1.552	3.132	3.282	0.225
249,000	249,999.9	1%	0.009	1.061	1.561	3.141	3.291	0.225
250,000	or more	0%	0.000	1.070	1.570	3.150	3.300	0.226

74

This is an example of a properly completed quarterly Excise Tax Return showing the use of the Small Domestic Wine Producer Credit in Schedule B:

What are the Rules for Transferring Small Domestic Wine Producer's Tax Credit?
26 U.S.C. 5041(c)(6) and 27 CFR 24.278-.279

Many small wine producers with limited space at their own wineries elect to transfer wine to other bonded wine premises (often commercial bonded wine cellars, or "BWCs") for storage and distribution. Small wineries often pay the excise tax on their wine before shipping it to a BWC, in order to make use of the Small Domestic Producer's Tax Credit. Under certain conditions, small wine producers have the option of transferring the use of their credit to other bonded wine premises, to be used when their wine is removed for consumption or sale (tax paid).

Who is eligible for the Small Domestic Producer's Credit?

Producers of not more than 250,000 gallons of wine per calendar year are eligible for a credit which lowers the tax due on the first 100,000 gallons of wine taxably removed each calendar year.

Non-producing wine premises and companies which produce more than 250,000 gallons per year are generally not eligible to use the Small Domestic Producer's Credit when making taxable removals from their bonded premises. The exception is when the credit is transferred by an eligible small producer to another taxpayer (a "transferee"), to be used on its behalf. A transferee is often a Bonded Wine Cellar (BWC), but it may be any bonded wine premises.

What wine is eligible for transfer of the Small Domestic Producer's Credit?

Credit may be transferred on wine (other than champagne or other sparkling wine) which was produced by a winery that is eligible for the credit.

When may a winery transfer its credit to another taxpayer?

There are five conditions which must be met before a transferee may use credit on behalf of an eligible small wine producer. All conditions must be met.

- The wine produced by the small winery would be eligible for the small domestic producer tax credit if removed from the producer's own premises.
- Wine is removed by the transferee, who is liable for the tax.
- The producer holds title to the wine at time of taxable removal.
- The producer provides to the transferee the information that is necessary to properly determine the transferee's credit.
- The removal is within the first 100,000 gallons taxably removed during the calendar year by the small winery and/or on behalf of the small winery.

76

What information should be sent to the transferee?

The transferee (receiver/taxpayer of the wine) needs enough information to properly determine how much credit to take. A written statement that includes the following would meet that need:

- The names of the producer and the transferee;
- The quantity and tax class of wines to be shipped;
- The date the wine is to be removed from bond for consumption or sale;.
- Confirmation that the producer is eligible for credit and the credit rate to which the wine is entitled (e.g., in the case of a blended wine, the percentage of wine, if any, that was not produced by the producer and is thus not eligible for the credit); and
- Confirmation that the shipment is within first 100,000 gallons removed by (or on behalf of) the producer for the calendar year.
- If not 100%, the percentage eligible for the credit

How is the Excise Tax Return Prepared?

The transferee uses that information to report and pay the taxes due. Here is an example of how to complete Schedule B of the Excise Tax Return, Form 5000.24, that shows how the tax to be paid was determined:

> The names of the producers for whom credit is being taken
> Their credit rates
> The total credit taken on behalf of each

Example of Schedule B

SCHEDULE B - ADJUSTMENTS DECREASING AMOUNT DUE		
EXPLANATION OF INDIVIDUAL ERRORS OR TRANSACTIONS	AMOUNT OF ADJUSTMENTS	
(a)	(b) TAX	(c) INTEREST
30. ABCD Cellars 2,377.5 gallons @ $.90 credit	$ 2,139.75	$
31. XYZ Vineyards, 59.4 gallons @ $ .72 credit	$ 42.77	
32.		
33. SUBTOTALS OF COLUMNS (b) and (c)	$ 2,182.52	$
34. TOTAL ADJUSTMENTS DECREASING AMOUNT DUE (Line 33, Col (b) + (c)) Enter here and on line 20.		$ 2,182.52

What does the producing winery show on its Reports and Returns?

The producing winery shows the transfer in bond to the transferee on its Report of Wine Premises Operations, Form 5120.17. It does not show the taxable removal on its tax returns or on its Report of Wine Premises Operations, Form 5120.17.

What does the transferee premises show on its Reports and Returns?

The transferee shows the receipt of wine transferred in bond from the producing winery on its Report of Wine Premises Operations, Form 5120.17. When the producer asks the transferee to make the taxable removal with its credit, the transferee shows the taxable removal of the wine from its Report of Wine Premises Operations, Form 5120.17 and files a tax return, listing the removal as shown above.

What is the limit for making taxable removals using the Small Domestic Producer's Credit?

The limit from all locations combined each calendar year is 100,000 wine gallons. The producer must keep track of all taxable removals being made on its behalf. After 100,000 gallons have been removed with credit from all locations, the producer's taxable removals must be made at the full rates (without credit) for the rest of the calendar year. This is why the transferee needs to receive written notice prior to each removal.

If the producer blends wine into its wine that it did not produce, can credit still be taken?

Yes and no. The credit is not transferable on wine which was not produced by the small producer. If wine was blended into the small producer's wine, the tax payment should be made at small producer's premises for full benefit of the credit.

The alternative is to notify the transferee in the written notice about the percentage of the wine which is ineligible for credit. The ineligible portion can then be taxpaid by the transferee at the full tax rate.

Can the producer transfer credit on wine it produced for a custom crush customer?

Yes, but only if the producer holds title to the wine at the time of removal from bond. If the custom crush customer holds title to the wine, the credit may not be transferred to another taxpayer. Accordingly, in order to get the benefit of the credit, the removal must be made from the producer's winery.

How are increasing and decreasing adjustments shown on the Excise Tax Return?

If, at the end of the calendar year, it is determined that the winery produced more wine than expected, making the credit rate which was used incorrect, all parties that have used the winery's small producer credit must make *increasing tax adjustments*.

Also, if the producer fails to produce any wine during the year, the taxpayers make an *increasing adjustment* during the last period of the calendar year.

If too much tax was paid on behalf of the producer, such as if the incorrect rate of credit was used, the transferees and any other taxpayers who used the winery's credit may file a claim on behalf of the producer. When the claim is approved by TTB, the taxpayers may make a *decreasing tax adjustment in the form of a credit, or request a refund.*

Summary of "Who Should Do What..."

1. Producer sends wine to transferee (i.e., BWC) with a transfer in bond record.

2. Producer shows wine has been transferred in bond on Form 5120.17.

3. Producer asks the transferee in writing to remove certain wine from bond.

4. Transferee shows taxable removal on its Form 5120.17 and pays the tax with producer's applicable credit rate.

5. Producer keeps track of how much wine has been taxably removed from any/all transferee facilities, keeping 100,000 total removals per year in mind.

6. Increasing or decreasing tax adjustments are made by the entities that taxably removed wine, and not the producer.

#

This is an example of a properly completed Excise Tax Return showing the use of <u>Transferred</u> Small Domestic Wine Producer Credit in Schedule B:

OMB No. 1513-0083 (04/30/2009)

DEPARTMENT OF THE TREASURY
ALCOHOL AND TOBACCO TAX AND TRADE BUREAU (TTB)
EXCISE TAX RETURN
(Prepare in duplicate – See instructions below)

1. SERIAL NUMBER	2010-8
3. AMOUNT OF PAYMENT	$ 27,649.93

NOTE: PLEASE MAKE CHECKS OR MONEY ORDERS PAYABLE TO THE ALCOHOL AND TOBACCO TAX AND TRADE BUREAU *(SHOW EMPLOYER IDENTIFICATION NUMBER ON ALL CHECKS OR MONEY ORDERS)*. IF YOU SEND A CHECK, SEE PAPER CHECK CONVERSION NOTICE BELOW.

2. FORM OF PAYMENT
[✓] CHECK [ ] MONEY ORDER [ ] EFT [ ] OTHER *(Specify)*_____

4. RETURN COVERS *(Check one)*
[ ] PREPAYMENT [✓] PERIOD
BEGINNING April 16, 2010
ENDING April 30, 2010

5. DATE PRODUCTS TO BE REMOVED *(For Prepayment Returns Only)*

6. EMPLOYER IDENTIFICATION NUMBER
94-987xxxx

7. PLANT, REGISTRY, OR PERMIT NUMBER
BWC-CA-xx10

8. NAME AND ADDRESS OF TAXPAYER *(Include ZIP Code)*
Thomson's Wine Storage
P.O. Box 63
Alloa, CA 9xxxx

FOR TTB USE ONLY
TAX	$
PENALTY	
INTEREST	
TOTAL	$
EXAMINED BY:	
DATE EXAMINED:	

CALCULATION OF TAX DUE *(Before making entries on lines 18 – 21, complete Schedules A and B)*

PRODUCT (a)	AMOUNT OF TAX (b)
9. DISTILLED SPIRITS	$
10. WINE	29,832.45
11. BEER	
12. CIGARS	
13. CIGARETTES	
14. CIGARETTE PAPERS AND/OR CIGARETTE TUBES	
15. CHEWING TOBACCO AND/OR SNUFF	
16. PIPE TOBACCO AND/OR ROLL-YOUR-OWN TOBACCO	
17. TOTAL TAX LIABILITY *(Total of lines 9-16)*	$ 29,832.45
18. ADJUSTMENTS INCREASING AMOUNT DUE *(From line 29)*	
19. GROSS AMOUNT DUE *(Line 17 plus line 18)*	$ 29,832.45
20. ADJUSTMENTS DECREASING AMOUNT DUE *(From line 34)*	2,182.52
21. AMOUNT TO BE PAID WITH THIS RETURN *(Line 19 minus line 20)*	$ 27,649.93

Under penalties of perjury, I declare that I have examined this return *(including any accompanying explanations, statements, schedules, and forms)* and to the best of my knowledge and belief it is true, correct, and includes all transactions and tax liabilities required by law or regulations to be reported.

22. DATE 5/14/2010	23. SIGNATURE *James M. Thomson*	24. TITLE General Manager

SCHEDULE A – ADJUSTMENTS INCREASING AMOUNT DUE

EXPLANATION OF INDIVIDUAL ERRORS OR TRANSACTIONS (a)	AMOUNT OF ADJUSTMENTS		
	(b) TAX	(c) INTEREST	(d) PENALTY
25.	$		$
26.			
27.			
28. SUBTOTALS OF COLUMNS (b), (c), and (d)	$	$	$
29. TOTAL ADJUSTMENTS INCREASING AMOUNT DUE *(Line 28, Col (b) + (c) + (d))* Enter here and on line 18.			$

SCHEDULE B – ADJUSTMENTS DECREASING AMOUNT DUE

EXPLANATION OF INDIVIDUAL ERRORS OR TRANSACTIONS (a)	AMOUNT OF ADJUSTMENTS	
	(b) TAX	(c) INTEREST
30. AB123 Cellars 2,377.5 gal, $.90/gal credit	$ 2,139.76	$
31. XYZ2 Winery, 59.4 gal, $.72/gal credit	42.77	
32.		
33. SUBTOTALS OF COLUMNS (b) and (c)	$ 2,182.52	$
34. TOTAL ADJUSTMENTS DECREASING AMOUNT DUE *(Line 33, Col (b) + (c))* Enter here and on line 20.		$ 2,182.52

Notice to Customers Making Payment by Check

If you send us a check, it will be converted into an electronic funds transfer (EFT). This means we will copy your check and use the account information on it to electronically debit your account for the amount of the check. The debit from your account will usually occur within 24 hours, and will be shown on your regular account statement.

You will not receive your original check back. We will destroy your original check, but we will keep the copy of it. If the EFT cannot be processed for technical reasons, you authorize us to process the copy in place of your original check. If the EFT cannot be completed because of insufficient funds, we may try to make the transfer up to 2 times.

TTB F 5000.24 (08/2007)

<u>Repeal of Special (Occupational) Tax on Alcohol Occupations</u>

On August 10, 2005, President Bush signed into law the "Safe, Accountable, Flexible, Efficient Transportation Equity Act: A Legacy for Users," Public Law 109-59. Section 11125 of the Act permanently repeals, effective July 1, 2008, the special (occupational) taxes on:

- Producers and marketers of alcohol beverages,
- Manufacturers of nonbeverage products,
- Users of tax-free alcohol, and
- Users and dealers of specially denatured spirits.

Although the tax has been repealed for these occupations, recordkeeping and registration requirements remain for:

- Producers and marketers of alcohol beverages, and
- Manufacturers of nonbeverage products.

Regulations will require marketers of alcohol beverages to register in the following circumstances:

- Before beginning business;
- On or before each subsequent July 1, but ONLY IF there has been a change in the existing registration information;
- Upon going out of business; and
- A transition rule will require the registration of existing businesses that have not registered on or after January 1, 2007.

Distilled spirits plants, breweries, wineries, bonded wine warehouses, and taxpaid wine bottling houses that sell alcohol products fit for beverage use will be treated as alcohol beverage dealers and therefore will be subject to the same registration requirements. However, to simplify the registration process, TTB will deem these persons to have registered as alcohol beverage dealers when they file their application for registration or brewer's notice under the qualification provisions of 27 CFR parts 19, 24, or 25. Similarly, amended dealer registrations will not be required if the qualification files are kept up to date.

Manufacturers of nonbeverage products will be deemed to have registered each year when they file their first claim for the year.

Recordkeeping requirements will remain as they are for:

- Alcohol beverage dealers,
- Manufacturers of nonbeverage products,
- Users of tax-free alcohol,
- Users and dealers of specially denatured spirits,
- Distilled spirits plants,
- Breweries,
- Wineries,
- Bonded wine warehouses, and
- Taxpaid wine bottling houses.

Any past due tax liabilities that were incurred for periods before the effective date of the repeal remain and will be collected. (However, there is no liability for alcohol occupations, other than users of tax-free alcohol and users and dealers of specially denatured spirits, during the previously enacted three-year tax suspension that runs from July 1, 2005, through June 30, 2008.)

Section 11125 of Public Law 109-59 does not affect any tobacco occupations; therefore,

- manufacturers of tobacco products,
- manufacturers of cigarette papers and tubes, and
- tobacco export warehouse proprietors

must continue to register and pay the special (occupational) tax every year. The registration and tax for these tobacco occupations is due before beginning business, and on or before July 1 of every year after that.

TTB plans to issue regulations amendments to implement the repeal as soon as possible. Corresponding changes will be made throughout the TTB Web site as appropriate.

See filing instructions and forms for current SOT requirements or call 1-800-937-8864 if you need additional assistance.

#

Notes

Federal Wine Labeling Regulations
📖 27 CFR Part 4

Subpart A   Scope
Subpart B   Definitions
Subpart C   Standards of Identity for Wine
Subpart D   Labeling Requirements for Wine
Subpart E   Requirements for Withdrawal of Wine from Customs Custody
Subpart F   Requirements for Approval of Labels of Wine Domestically Bottled or Packed
Subpart G   Advertising of Wine
Subpart H   Standards of Fill for Wine
Subpart I   General Provisions
Subpart J   American Grape Variety Names
Subpart K   Use of the term "Organic"

Part 4, Subpart C – Standards of Identity for Wine

4.20   Application of standards.
4.21   The standards of identity.
4.22   Blends, cellar treatment, alteration of class or type.
4.23   Varietal (grape type) labeling.
4.24   Generic, semi-generic, and non-generic designations of geographic significance.
4.25   Appellations of origin.
4.26   Estate bottled.
4.27   Vintage wine.
4.28   Type designations of varietal significance.

Part 4, Subpart D – Labeling Requirements for Wine

4.30   General.
4.32   Mandatory label information.
4.32a   Voluntary disclosure of major food allergens
4.32b   Petitions for exemption from major food allergen labeling
4.33   Brand names.
4.34   Class and type.
4.35   Name and address.
4.36   Alcoholic content.
4.37   Net contents.
4.38   General requirements.
4.38   Bottle cartons, booklets and leaflets.
4.39   Prohibited practices.

Wine Labeling

1. Labels must be pre-approved by TTB (27 CFR 4.50(a))

2. Mandatory Label Information (27 CFR 4.32)

<u>Brand Label:</u>

Brand Name (27 CFR 4.33)

Class or Type Designation (27 CFR 4.34)

Alcohol Content (27 CFR 4.36)

<u>Any Label:</u>

Bottler's Name and Address (27 CFR 4.35)

Net Contents (27 CFR 4.37)

Sulfite Declaration (27 CFR 4.32(e))

Health Warning Statement (27 CFR 16)

Brand Name
27 CFR 4.33

The Brand Label must bear a Brand Name (the name under which the product is sold).

If there is no Brand Name, the name of the bottler, packer or importer, if shown on the Brand Label, is considered the Brand Name.

The Brand Name may not create a misleading impression about the product.

Class and Type Designations
27 CFR 4.21 and 4.34

The "class and type" is the specific identity of the wine, and it must appear on the Brand Label.

Nine classes are listed in 27 CFR 4.21:

> Grape Wine
> Sparkling Grape Wine
> Carbonated Grape Wine
> Citrus Wine
> Fruit Wine
> Wine from Other Agricultural Products
> Aperitif Wine
> Imitation and Substandard or Other than Standard Wine
> Retsina Wine

An Appellation of Origin must appear in direct conjunction with, and in lettering substantially as conspicuous as, the class and type designation, if a varietal, a type designation of varietal significance, a semi-generic designation or a vintage date is used. (27 CFR 4.34(b))

Alcohol Content
27 CFR 4.36

- The alcohol content statement must appear on the Brand Label. Alcohol content may also appear on a strip label, if it appears with the brand label.

- Wines with an alcohol content of 14% or less may be stated as "Table" wine or with the alcoholic content.

- If the alcoholic content is used, it must appear as the percentage of alcohol by volume:

  "Alcohol ___% by volume"

- If a range is used, it may read: "Alcohol ___% to ___% by volume"

- Abbreviations may be used for "Alcohol" and "Volume:"

  "Alc." or "Alc"
  "Vol." or "Vol"

- Tolerances :

  1.5% for wines with 14% or less alcohol by volume; may not cross into the next tax class

  1% for wines with more than 14% alcohol by volume; may not cross into a different tax class

  3% when a range is shown on 14% or less alcohol wines; must be within the stated range

  2% when a range is shown on more than 14% alcohol wines; must be within the stated range

- Examples of alcohol test results

Test Result	Tax Class
13.999%	14% and under
14.0000%	14% and under
14.01% to 14.04%	14% and under
14.05% to 14.09%	Over 14%
14.1% Over	14%

Bottler's Name and Address
27 CFR 4.35

1. Name of the bottler, and City and State as shown on the Basic Permit or other qualification document.

2. Must be preceded by "Bottled by" or "Packed by"

3. Additional statements that may be used:

   - "Produced" or "Made" may be used if the bottling winery -

     Fermented not less than 75% of the wine at the stated address, or

     Changed the class or type of the wine at the stated address, or

     Produced sparkling wine by secondary fermentation at the stated address

   - "Blended" may be used if the named winery mixed the wine with other wines of the same class and type at the stated address

   - "Cellared," "Vinted" or "Prepared" may be used if the named winery subjected the wine to cellar treatment at the stated address

4. The operating or trade name used must be identical to a name listed on the Basic Permit or other qualification document.

Net Contents
27 CFR 4.37, 27 CFR 4.72; 27 CFR 24.255(b)

Must be stated in metric standard of fill using milliliters or "ml" on containers of less than one liter, and as liters and decimal portions of a liter on containers of one liter or more. May be etched or blown into the glass in lieu of appearing on the label, and U.S. equivalents may also be shown.

Metric Standards of Fill:

3 liters	750 milliliters	187 milliliters	Even liters for
1 liter	500 milliliters 100	milliliters cont	ainers of 4 liters
375	milliliters	50 milliliters	or larger.

Fill tolerances are listed in 27 CFR 24.255(b) (see page 125).

Sulfite Declaration
27 CFR 4.32(e)

The Sulfite Declaration must appear as "Contains Sulfites," "Contains (a) Sulfiting Agent(s)," or similar appropriate phrase.

It is required if total sulfur dioxide or a sulfating agent is detected at 10 ppm or more.

The statement may be omitted if laboratory analysis determines that the sulfite content is less than 10 ppm total sulfur dioxide.   The analysis may be performed by TTB or by a TTB-Certified Laboratory.

Attach the lab analysis to Form 5100.31 Application for Certificate of Label Approval when you send it for approval.

Call the TTB Compliance Laboratory in Walnut Creek, CA about the submission of samples:

(925) 280-3642

Alcohol Beverage Health Warning Statement
27 CFR Part 16

The statement must appear on all containers for sale or distribution, must be legible on a contrasting background, and appear separate and apart from all other information.

The words "**GOVERNMENT WARNING**" must appear in capital letters and in bold type, and the rest of the warning statement may not appear in bold type. The "S" in "Surgeon" and the "G" in General must also be capitalized.

Required language:

GOVERNMENT WARNING:
(1) According to the Surgeon General, women should not drink alcoholic beverages during pregnancy because of the risk of birth defects.
(2) Consumption of alcoholic beverages impairs your ability to drive a car or operate machinery, and may cause health problems.

Fruit Wine
27 CFR 4.21(e)

Fruit wine derived wholly from one kind of fruit shall be designated by the word "**wine**" qualified by the name of such fruit **[e.g., "peach wine," "blackberry wine"]**.

Berry wine is fruit wine produced from berries.

Fruit wine or *berry wine* derived from more than one fruit may be designated as Fruit Wine or Berry Wine qualified by a truthful and adequate statement of composition appearing in direct conjunction. If any fruit contributes less than 40% to the blend of two fruits, less than 30% to a blend of three fruits, or less than 20% to a blend of four fruits, percentages must be shown for each fruit, totaling 100%.

Fruit table wine or *berry table wine* is fruit or berry wine having an alcoholic content not in excess of 14 percent by volume.

Fruit dessert wine or *berry dessert wine* is fruit or berry wine having an alcoholic content in excess of 14 percent but not in excess of 24 percent by volume.

Any fruit wine containing no added brandy or alcohol may be further designated as "**natural**."

Formula Wines
27 CFR 24.80

The proprietor shall, before production, obtain approval of the formula and process by which special natural wine, agricultural wine, and other than standard wine are to be made. [e.g., Honey Wine; Rhubarb Wine; Blend of Grape and Peach Wine]

The formula must be prepared and filed on TTB F 5100.51, Formula and Process for Domestic and Imported Alcohol Beverages.

Qualifications on an approved wine formula may require additional labeling.

Examples:

- "Other than Standard Wine"
- "Grape Wine with Artificial Flavors Added"
- "Grape Wine with Natural Flavor Added"
- "A Blend of Grape Wine and ["Name of Fruit"] Wine"
  (Label must show percentage of each kind of wine)

Hard Cider

In accordance with 27 CFR 24.10, Hard Cider ~

- Is a still wine derived primarily from apples or apple concentrate and water (apple juice, or the equivalent amount of concentrate reconstituted to the original brix of the juice prior to concentration, must represent more than 50 percent of the volume of the finished product)

- Contains no other fruit product nor any artificial product which imparts a fruit flavor other than apple

- Contains at least one-half of 1 percent and less than 7 percent alcohol by volume

- Has the taste, aroma and characteristics generally attributed to hard cider

- Is sold or offered for sale as hard cider

Excise Tax on Hard Cider: $ .226 per wine gallon (26 USC 5041(b)(6))

Small Domestic Wine Producer Credit on Hard Cider: For producers of not more than 150,000 gallons of wines during the calendar year, the credit on hard cider is $.056 per wine gallon for the first 100,000 gallons of wine taxably removed per calendar year. The credit is reduced for producers of more than 150,000 gallons but not more than 250,000 gallons of wine. Production and taxable removal of hard cider is counted along with other types of wine for determining eligibility for small domestic wine producer credit.

Labeling: Since the term "hard cider" designates a wine tax class defined in 27 CFR Part 24.10 (as paraphrased above), but may also be used on the labels of wines that do not belong to that tax class (such as fruit-flavored hard ciders or apple wine containing 7% or more alcohol by volume), the wine must be adequately marked to identify the tax class. See also 27 CFR 4.21(e)(5), Standards of Identity, Class 5, fruit wine, and 27 CFR 24.257(a)(4)(iv), Labeling Wine Containers.

Records and Reports: Wine records are maintained by tax class and must include a separate record for hard cider, if produced, received, etc. The Report of Wine Premises Operations Form 5120.17 provides a separate column for the reporting of hard cider production, receipt and removal.

Minimum Type Sizes
27 CFR 4.38; 27 CFR 16.22

Brand Name, Class/Type, Bottler's Name and Address, Net Contents, Sulfite Statement and Appellation (if mandatory):

At least 2 mm for containers larger than 187 ml;
At least 1 mm for containers 187 ml or less

Alcohol content:

At least 1 mm but not larger than 3 mm for containers of less than 5 L

Health Warning Statement:

- Not smaller than 3 mm for containers larger than 3L with a maximum of 12 characters per inch

- Not smaller than 2 mm for containers over 237 ml to 3L with a maximum of 25 characters per inch

- Not smaller than 1 mm for containers of 237 ml or less with a maximum of 40 characters per inch

Optional Labeling Terms

Varietal Designation   One   variety: 75%
27 CFR 4.23, 4.28, 4.91   Name is listed in 27 CFR 4.91
    Appellati   on of Origin
    Entire   75% varietal content comes
    from   named Appellation
    Two   or more varieties: % of each

Appellation of Origin   75% for a Political Subdivision
27 CFR 4.25   85% for an American Viticultural Area
    (AVA)

Estate Bottled   Winery grew 100% of the grapes and
27 CFR 4.26   produced and bottled 100% of the
    wine,   and the grapes were harvested
    from   vineyard(s) in the same AVA as
    the   bottling winery.
    Appellation must be an AVA.

Vintage Date   95%   from year of harvest if an AVA is
27 CFR 4.27   used as the Appellation
    85% if an AVA is not used as the
    Appellation
    Appellati   on must be smaller than a
    country

Produced or Made By   75% produced by fermentation or
27 CFR 4.35   Class/type was changed by bottler

Vineyard Designation   95%   from grapes harvested from
27 CFR 4.39(m)   named   vineyard

Appellation of Origin
27 CFR 4.25

An appellation of origin is required to appear on the Brand label if any of the following appear on your label:

- Grape varietal is used on the Brand label
- Type designation of varietal significance is used on the Brand label
- Semi-generic designation
- Vintage date
- Estate Bottled (AVA required)

An American appellation may be:

- United States
  - At least 75% of the wine is derived from fruit grown in the United States and the wine is fully finished in the United States
- A   State
  - At least 75% of the wine is derived from fruit grown in the State and the wine is fully finished within the State or adjoining State
- Two or no more than three contiguous States
  - All of the fruit was grown in the States indicated, the percentage of wine from each State is shown and the wine is fully finished in one of the labeled appellation States
- A   County
  - At least 75% of the wine is derived from fruit grown in the county and the wine is fully finished within the State where the county is located
- Two or no more than three Counties (in the same State)
  - All of the fruit was grown in the counties indicated, the percentage of wine from each county is shown and the wine is fully finished in the State where the counties are located
- American Viticultural Area (AVA)
  - The appellation has been approved by the TTB
  - At least 85% of the wine is derived from grapes grown within the boundaries of the viticultural area and the wine is fully finished in the State where the viticultural area is located
- Overlappin g AVA's
  - An appellation of more than one AVA may be used if the AVA's overlap and not less than 85% of the volume of the wine is derived from grapes grown in the overlapping area

Wines Made From Out-of-State Fruit
27 CFR 4.39 and 27 CFR 24.314

Statements on labels must be truthful and supported by a complete and accurate audit trail. A wine is not entitled to have information stated on the label unless the information can be readily verified by a complete and accurate record trail from the beginning source material to removal of the wine for consumption or sale.

Example 1: Wine made by an Idaho winery by fermentation of <u>juice</u> from at least 75% Chardonnay grapes grown in Washington in 2006, could be labeled:

- 2006 Washington Chardonnay, produced/bottled by ID winery; or
- A<u>merican</u> Chardonnay, produced/bottled by ID winery

Example 2: Wine made by an Idaho winery by blending 25% <u>wine</u> produced by their own fermentation with 75% Chardonnay <u>wine</u> produced in Washington from 2006 grapes and shipped in bond, could be labeled:

- 2006 Washington Chardonnay, Vinted and bottled by ID winery; or
- A<u>merican</u> Chardonnay, Vinted and bottled by ID winery

Example 3: Wine made by an Idaho winery by fermentation of <u>juice</u> from <u>less than</u> 75% Chardonnay grapes grown in Washington in 2006 could be labeled:

- White Wine, produced and bottled by ID winery

Example 4: Wine made by an Idaho winery by fermentation of <u>juice</u> from at least 75% Chardonnay grapes grown in California in 2006, could be labeled:

- A<u>merican</u> Chardonnay, produced/bottled by ID winery

Labeling Imported Bottled Wine

1. Labels must be pre-approved by TTB (27 CFR 4.40)

2. Mandatory Label Information (27 CFR 4.32)

   <u>Brand Label:</u>

   Brand Name (27 CFR 4.33)

   Class or Type Designation (27 CFR 4.34)

   Alcohol Content (27 CFR 4.36)

   Appellation (27 CFR 4.23 - 4.27). under certain circumstances

   <u>Any Label:</u>

   Importer's Name and Address (27 CFR 4.35 (b))

   Net Contents (27 CFR 4.37)

   Sulfite Declaration (27 CFR 4.32(e))

   Health Warning Statement (27 CFR 16)

   Country of Origin
   (U.S. Customs and Border Protection requirement)

Labeling Imported Bulk Wine

1) Bulk wine must be imported by the holder of a Federal Importer's Basic Permit.

2) For blends of American and foreign wines:

- The percentage of foreign wine must be disclosed if any reference is made to presence of the foreign wine

- The blend must conform to country of origin's requirements

- If the blend is less than 75% American or Foreign, no appellation of origin, vintage or varietal designation may be shown

- If the blend is at least 75% American
  - May be labeled with "American" and have a varietal designation
  - May be labeled with an appellation other than American, if:
    - Wine meets applicable percentage requirements (75% or 85%)
    - Wine is fully finished in labeled appellation
    - Wine conforms to laws and regulations of labeled appellation.

- If the blend is at least 75% Foreign, the wine may be labeled with the Foreign appellation if the wine conforms to the requirements of the Foreign laws and regulations governing the composition, method of production, and designation of wines available for consumption within the country of origin

- "Country of origin" label statement may be required on bulk wine imported and bottled in the U.S. (USCBP requirement)

3) For 100% Foreign Wine Bottled in the U.S.:

- The wine may be labeled with foreign appellation of origin only if it meets appropriate percentage requirements for appellations under TTB's regulations, and it meets laws and regulations of the labeled appellation of origin.

- If the wine is **not** labeled with an appellation, it may not be labeled with a vintage or varietal designation.

- "Country of origin" label statement may be required on bulk wine imported and bottled in the U.S. (USCBP requirement)

4) Contact TTB's International Trade Division for further advice at (202) 453-2260.

Organic Labeling

❖ The National Organic Program (NOP) is administered by the U.S. Dept. of Agriculture (7 CFR Part 205).

See   www.ams.usda.gov/nop for information on requirements.

❖ As of May 23, 2005, all organic labeling applicants who are certified by a USDA-accredited certifying agent (ACA) must obtain their ACA's review and approval of their organic labels prior to submission to TTB. Documented proof of ACA review must accompany the COLA when submitted to TTB.

Proof of ACA review will be accepted in the form of a letter or memorandum from the ACA, which must include a copy of the alcohol beverage label signed and dated by the ACA.

Any such application received in TTB from a certified entity without proof of ACA review will be automatically rejected.

Notes

Descriptive Terms of Specialized Farming Practices Other than *Organic*

Description of specialized farming practices other than "organic" may appear on alcohol beverage labels as additional information provided it is truthful, accurate, specific, and does not conflict with mandatory labeling information per 27 CFR 4.38 (f) and 4.39(a)(1). TTB neither defines nor regulates specialized farming terms but does reserve the right to request clarification and documented verification of any graphics, seals, logos, or descriptive language appearing on labels.

ALFD has determined that valid certifying documents are required when the following terms and/or logos appear on labels:

- Agriculture Biologique" or "Biodynamic" appearing on labels in any manner .
- "Biodyvin" or the accompanying logo appearing on the label. This is an actual French certifier of biodynamic wines.
- "L.I.V.E." anagram (Low Impact Viticulture and Enology) appears on label as a logo or in text.
- Certified Fair Trade or Fair Trade

Any label specifically stating that the producer is certified by an agricultural organization must have documented proof.

The following terms do not require certification and may appear on the label in combination with words such as "Viticulture", "Farming", "Farmed", "Ecology", and "Agriculture":

- All Natural, Natural, Naturally – May not appear on flavored products
- Sustainable, Sustainably
- Dolphin Safe
- Salmon Safe
- Fish Friendly Farming

The following terms usually pertain to the environmental impact of the process and packaging rather than to the product itself. These words and phrases may not modify mandatory information on brand labels, but might appear as additional information after review on a case-by-case basis:

- Eco-Friendly
- Environmentally Friendly

- Carbon Zero – with further clarification
- Carbon Neutral
- Carbon Footprint
- Green

The following descriptive terms are generally misleading and are prohibited from appearing on alcohol beverage labels (note that this is not an all-inclusive list):

- Contains No GMOs
- GMO Free (such as GMO Free Mendocino County)
- GMO Free-Zone
- GMO (Genetically Modified Organism)
- Not Genetically Modified
- Carbon Free
- Sulfite Free

DEPARTMENT OF THE TREASURY
Alcohol and Tobacco Tax and Trade Bureau

<u>Industry Circular 2006-1</u>
Date: March 10, 2006

Impact of the U.S./EU Wine Agreement on Certificates of Label Approval for Wine Labels with a Semi-Generic Name or Retsina

To: Bonded Wineries, Bonded Wine Cellars, Taxpaid Wine Bottling Houses, Importers, and Others Concerned.

Purpose

This circular:

- Explains the intended change regarding who may use semi-generic names and Retsina on wine labels;

- Explains the expected conditions under which semi-generic names and Retsina may be used on non-EU wine labels;

- Provides guidance on how to submit applications for certificate of label approval (COLA) for wine labels that contain semi-generic names and Retsina; and

- Explains the qualification that appears on your COLA for wine labels with a semi-generic name or Retsina issued on or after March 10, 2006.

Summary

Following several years of negotiations, the United States and the European Union (EU) signed an agreement on trade in wine between the parties ("the Agreement") on March 10, 2006. The Agreement addresses a wide range of issues regarding the production, labeling, and import requirements for wine that help to establish predictable conditions for bilateral wine trade. Most significantly for U.S. wine exporters, the Agreement replaces the temporary, short-term derogations the EU has been renewing since 1983 to allow the importation of U.S. wine made using practices not recognized by EU regulations. The Agreement also addresses semi-generic names of origin and the class designation Retsina when they are used on non-EU wine, that is, U.S. wine and wine from other non-EU countries that is sold in the U.S. You may view the full text of the Agreement via the TTB Web site.

Note: As of the date of this circular, the EU is comprised of 25 member States. They are:

Austria Latvia		
Belgium Lithuania		
Cyprus Luxembourg		
Czech Republic	Malta	
Denmark Poland		
Estonia Portugal		
Finland Slovak	Republic	
France Slovenia		
Germany Spain		
Greece Sweden		
Hungary	the Netherlands	
Ireland United	Kingdom	
Italy		

Semi-Generic Names

The Internal Revenue Code of 1986 (IRC) at 26 U.S.C. 5388(c) defines each semi-generic name as a name of geographic significance that is also a designation of class and type for wine. The IRC further states that a semi-generic name may be used to designate wine of an origin other than that indicated by its name only if there appears, in direct conjunction with the designation, an appropriate appellation of origin disclosing the true place of origin and the wine so designated conforms to the standard of identity. The semi-generic names and the place of origin indicated by each name are:

Burgundy (France)	Malaga (Spain)
Chablis (France)	Marsala (Italy)
Champagne (France)	Moselle (France)
Chianti (Italy)	Port (Portugal)
Claret (France)	Rhine (Germany)
Haut Sauterne (France)	Sauterne (France)
Hock (Germany)	Sherry (Spain)
Madeira (Portugal)	Tokay (Hungary)

Note: Angelica is a semi-generic name for wine of U.S. origin; however, the Agreement does not affect its use, and it is not subject to any of the information in this circular.

Retsina

Retsina is a class of wine and is not a semi-generic name; however, under the terms of the Agreement, it is treated the same as the semi-generic names. Its origin is Greece.

Background

In the Agreement, the U.S. made a commitment to seek to change the legal status of the semi-generic names and of Retsina to restrict their use solely to wines originating in the applicable EU member state, with certain exceptions. Because the IRC specifically defines semi-generic names, this law must be changed in order to restrict the usage of the names to wines originating in the EU. Assuming the law is so changed, the Agreement contains an exception to this rule. We refer to this exception as the "grandfather" provision. Under the "grandfather" provision, any person or his or her successor in interest may continue to use a semi-generic name or Retsina on a label of a wine not originating in the EU, *provided* the semi-generic name or Retsina is only used on labels for wine bearing the same brand name, or the brand name and the fanciful name, if any, that appear on a COLA that was issued prior to March 10, 2006.

Note: As of the publication date of this circular, the IRC has not yet been changed. The Alcohol and Tobacco Tax and Trade Bureau (TTB) will update this circular to reflect any relevant changes made to the IRC by statute.

Example

In order to further your understanding of this issue we offer the following scenario. In this example it is assumed that:

- The wine conforms to the standard of identity for Sherry, and

- The law has been changed to conform to our commitment in the Agreement.

Company A produces "Smith Elegance California Cream Sherry." On the label and corresponding COLA, the brand name is "Smith," the fanciful name is "Elegance," "Sherry" is the class and type designation and "California" is the labeled appellation of origin. (Sherry that is not from Spain must be labeled with an appellation of origin.)

- Under the "grandfather" provision, Company A may continue to use the semi-generic name "Sherry" on labels, *provided* they do not change the brand name or fanciful name as they appear on a COLA that was issued before March 10, 2006.

However:

- If Company A changes the brand name from "Smith" to "Jones," the use of the semi-generic name "Sherry" *is not* "grandfathered" and *is not* permitted.

- If Company A continues to use the brand name "Smith" but changes the fanciful name from "Elegance" to "Robust," the use of the semi-generic name "Sherry" *is not* "grandfathered" and *is not* permitted.

- If Company A continues to use the brand name "Smith" and the fanciful name "Elegance" and changes the appellation of origin from "California" to "Napa Valley," the use of the semi-generic name "Sherry" *is* "grandfathered" and *is* permitted.

- If Company A continues to use the brand name "Smith" and the fanciful name "Elegance" and deletes "Cream," the use of the semi-generic name "Sherry" *is* "grandfathered" and *is* permitted.

- If Company A sells the rights to *Smith Elegance California Cream Sherry* to Company B, all the same rights and restrictions apply to Company B or any future owner of the brand.

<u>Note:</u> It is sometimes difficult to identify the brand name and the fanciful name by simply viewing the label. If there is any question of eligibility for the "grandfather" provision, we will rely on the information that appears in the "Brand Name" and "Fanciful Name" fields on the COLA that was approved before March 10, 2006.

COLAs with Semi-Generic Names or Retsina Submitted On or After March 10, 2006.

In order to facilitate the review of COLAs for wine labels that contain semi-generic names or Retsina and for the U.S. to uphold its commitments in the Agreement, we instituted the following procedures and we ask for your cooperation. Providing the requested information assists us in processing your application in the timeliest fashion. Failure to provide the requested information may result in your application being rejected or returned for correction.

- If your COLA is for a "new" use of a semi-generic name or Retsina, that is, no COLA was issued before March 10, 2006, for this semi-generic name or Retsina that reflects the same brand name or brand name and fanciful name, if any, please attach a note to your application stating "This application is for a new use of the semi-generic name (specify name) or Retsina" (as applicable).

  <u>Note:</u> Pending any change to the law, TTB will continue to approve "new" uses of the semi-generic names and Retsina. Please keep in mind that in order for the U.S. to meet its obligations in the Agreement, the Government must seek to change the law to limit the use of these names on non-EU wine to those brands that were in existence before March 10, 2006.

- If your COLA is for a "grandfathered" brand of semi-generic wine or Retsina, that is, there is a COLA issued before March 10, 2006, with the same semi-generic name or Retsina and the same brand name or brand name and fanciful name, if any, please include with your COLA application a copy of either the COLA that was issued before March 10, 2006, or a COLA with a qualification that confirms that it is for a "grandfathered" brand. We recognize that the COLA submitted in support of your application may not have been issued to your company. For example, if Company B purchased rights to Company A's "grandfathered" brand name, Company B may submit a copy of Company A's COLA to support its application.

Qualifications on COLAs

In order to provide you with guidance and information about your labels, we apply a qualification to COLAs with semi-generic names and Retsina issued on or after March 10, 2006. We desire to give applicants for "new" uses, that is, for brands for which no COLA was issued prior to March 10, 2006, advance notice that the U.S. Government is committed to seeking a change in the law regarding the use of these names that may affect the labels on the COLA. Qualifying COLAs for "grandfathered" brands helps to streamline the review of future COLA submissions for these brands.

- COLAs for "new" uses of the semi-generic names or Retsina are qualified:

"As per the Agreement Between the U.S. and EU on Trade in Wine, the U.S. is seeking to change 26 U.S.C. 5388(c) regarding the use of semi-generic names and Retsina to limit their use to wine solely from the applicable EU member country unless used on a COLA before March 10, 2006. If enacted, this change will result in this certificate being revoked by operation of law (27 CFR 13.51)."

- COLAs for "grandfathered" brands that use a semi-generic name or Retsina are qualified:

"Approved under the "grandfather" provision of the Agreement between the U.S. and the EU on Trade in Wine."

Questions

If you have questions concerning this circular, please contact the Advertising, Labeling and Formulation Division (ALFD) at 1-866-927-ALFD (2533) or alfd@ttb.gov.

John J. Manfreda
Administrator
Alcohol and Tobacco Tax and Trade Bureau

Department of the Treasury | **Alcohol and Tobacco Tax and Trade Bureau**

TTB Press Release

For Immediate Release
Contact: Art Resnick (202)927-8062

December 20, 2006
FY-07-07

COLAS REVOKED FOR CERTAIN SEMI-GENERIC NAMES

Washington. D.C. - On March 10, 2006, the U.S. and the European Union (EU) signed an Agreement on Trade in Wine in which the U.S. committed to seek to change the legal status of certain semi-generic names to restrict their use solely to wine originating in the applicable EU member state, except as provided for under a "grandfather" provision. These names, along with Retsina, are: Burgundy, Claret, Chablis, Champagne, Chianti, Malaga, Marsala, Madeira, Moselle, Port, Rhine Wine or Hock, Sauterne, Haut Sauterne, Sherry, and Tokay. The "grandfather" provision excepts certain non-EU wines labeled with a semi-generic name or Retsina provided the applicable label was approved on a certificate of label approval (COLA) or certificate of exemption issued before March 10, 2006. For more details, see TTB Industry Circular 2006-1 on our web site at www.ttb.gov.

A legislative proposal that will effect the change in legal status of the EU semi-generic names and Retsina was included in Tax Relief and Health Care Act of 2006 that was enacted on December 20, 2006. Enactment of this legislation means that any COLA or certificate of exemption for a non-EU wine with a semi-generic name or Retsina that was not approved under the "grandfather" provision is subject to immediate revocation by operation of law.

How can you tell if your COLA or certificate of exemption is subject to revocation? You can tell by the qualification statement that appears on the COLA or certificate of exemption. Beginning March 10, 2006, the Alcohol and Tobacco Tax and Trade Bureau (TTB) earmarked those COLAs and certificates of exemption that would be affected if the legislative change occurred by qualifying them with the statement:

> "As per the Agreement Between the U.S. and EC on Trade in Wine, the U.S. is seeking to change 26 U.S.C. 5388(c) regarding the use of semi-generic names and Retsina to limit their use to wines solely from the applicable EU member country unless used on a COLA prior to 03/10/2006. If enacted, this change will result in this certificate being revoked by operation of law (27 CFR 13.51)."

As a result of the recently-enacted law further use of any COLAs or certificates of exemption bearing the above qualification by TTB must cease. However, products which have been bottled or imported before December 20, 2006, may still be removed from bond.

Questions regarding this issue should be directed to the Advertising, Labeling and Formulation Division (ALFD). ALFD can be reached at (202) 927-8140 or toll free at 1-(866) 927-2533 or by e-mail at ALFD@TTB.gov.

#####

Prohibited Labeling Practices
27 CFR 4.39

27 CFR 4.39(a): Statements on labels. Containers of wine, or any label…shall not contain:

1) False, untrue or misleading statements
2) Statements disparaging to competitor's products
3) Obscene or indecent statements, designs, devices
4) Statements regarding analyses, standards, tests which may be misleading
5) Statements regarding guarantees which may be misleading (money-back guarantees OK)
6) Fal se endorsements
7) Statements creating an impression the product contains spirits or is a spirits product
8) False entitlement to class or type designations
9) Distilled spirits-type names

Other prohibitions related to the following are found in…

27 CFR 4.39(b): Statement of age
    4.39(c): Statement of bottling dates
    4.39(d): Statement of miscellaneous dates
    4.39(e): Simulation of Government stamps
    4.39(f): Use of the word "Importer" or similar words
    4.39(g): Flags, seals, coats of arms, crests and other insignia
    4.39(h): Health Related Statements
    4.39(I): Geographic brand names
    4.39(j): Product names of geographic significance
    4.39(k): Other indications of origin
    4.39(l): Foreign terms
    4.39(m): Use of a vineyard, orchard, farm or ranch name unless 95%
    4.39(n): Use of a varietal name, type designation of varietal significance,   semi-generic name, or geographic distinctive designation

Prohibited Advertising Practices
27 CFR 4.64

27 CFR 4.64(a) Restrictions: The advertisement of wine shall not contain:

1) False, untrue or misleading statements
2) Statements disparaging to competitor's products
3) Obscene or indecent statements, designs, devices, representations
4) Statements, designs, devices, representations of analyses, standards, tests which may be misleading
5) Statements, designs, devices, representations regarding guarantees which may be misleading (money-back guarantees are OK)
6) Any statement that the wine is produced, blended, bottled, packed, sold under any government authorization, supervision or standard
7) Any statement of bonded winery or bonded wine cellar number, unless in direct conjunction with the name and address of the operator
8) Statements, designs, devices, representations creating an impression the product contains spirits, is comparable to a distilled spirit, or has intoxicating qualities
9) Distilled spirits-type brand names

Other prohibitions are found in 27 CFR Part 4.64, as follows:

4.64(b): Statements inconsistent with labeling (only approved labels may be depicted in an advertisement)
4.64(c): Statement of age
4.64(d): Statement of bottling dates
4.64(e): Statement of miscellaneous dates
4.64(f): Flags, seals, coats of arms, crests, other insignia
4.64(g): Statements indicative of origin
4.64(h): Use of the word "importer" or similar words
4.64(i): Health-related statements
4.64(j): Confusion of brands
4.64(k): Deceptive advertising techniques

OMB No. 1513-0020 (01/31/2009)

FOR TTB USE ONLY

TTB ID

DEPARTMENT OF THE TREASURY
ALCOHOL AND TOBACCO TAX AND TRADE BUREAU
APPLICATION FOR AND CERTIFICATION/EXEMPTION OF
LABEL/BOTTLE APPROVAL
(See Instructions and Paperwork Reduction Act Notice Below)

1. REP. ID. NO. *(If any)*   CT   OR

PART I - APPLICATION

2. PLANT REGISTRY/BASIC PERMIT/BREWER'S NO. *(Required)*

3. SOURCE OF PRODUCT *(Required)*
☐ Domestic   ☐ Imported

8. NAME AND ADDRESS OF APPLICANT AS SHOWN ON PLANT REGISTRY, BASIC PERMIT, OR BREWER'S NOTICE. INCLUDE APPROVED DBA OR TRADENAME IF USED ON THE LABEL *(Required)*

4. SERIAL NUMBER *(Required)*
YEAR -

5. TYPE OF PRODUCT *(Required)*
☐ WINE
☐ DISTILLED SPIRITS
☐ MALT BEVERAGES

8a. MAILING ADDRESS, IF DIFFERENT

6. BRAND NAME *(Required)*

7. FANCIFUL NAME *(If any)*

9. E-MAIL ADDRESS

10. FORMULA/SOP NO. *(If any)*

11. LAB. NO. & DATE/PRE-IMPORT NO. & DATE *(If any)*

18. TYPE OF APPLICATION *(Check applicable box(es))*
a. ☐ CERTIFICATE OF LABEL APPROVAL
b. ☐ CERTIFICATE OF EXEMPTION FROM LABEL APPROVAL
   "For sale in _____ only" (Fill in State abbreviation)
c. ☐ DISTINCTIVE LIQUOR BOTTLE APPROVAL. TOTAL BOTTLE CAPACITY BEFORE CLOSURE_____
   (Fill in amount)
d. ☐ RESUBMISSION AFTER REJECTION
   TTB ID _____

12. NET CONTENTS

13. ALCOHOL CONTENT

14. WINE APPELLATION *(If on label)*

15. WINE VINTAGE DATE *(If on label)*

16. PHONE NUMBER

17. FAX NUMBER

19. SHOW ANY WORDING (a) APPEARING ON MATERIALS FIRMLY AFFIXED TO THE CONTAINER *(e.g., caps, celoseals, corks, etc.)* OTHER THAN THE LABELS AFFIXED BELOW, OR (b) BLOWN, BRANDED, OR EMBOSSED ON THE CONTAINER *(e.g., net contents, etc.)*. THIS WORDING MUST BE NOTED HERE EVEN IF IT DUPLICATES PORTIONS OF THE LABELS AFFIXED BELOW. ALSO, PROVIDE TRANSLATIONS OF FOREIGN LANGUAGE TEXT APPEARING ON LABELS.

PART II - APPLICANT'S CERTIFICATION

Under the penalties of perjury, I declare: that all statements appearing on this application are true and correct to the best of my knowledge and belief; and, that the representations on the labels attached to this form, including supplemental documents, truly and correctly represent the content of the containers to which these labels will be applied. I also certify that I have read, understood, and complied with the conditions and instructions which are attached to an original TTB F 5100.31, Certificate/Exemption of Label/Bottle Approval.

20. DATE OF APPLICATION

21. SIGNATURE OF APPLICANT OR AUTHORIZED AGENT

22. PRINT NAME OF APPLICANT OR AUTHORIZED AGENT

PART III - TTB CERTIFICATE

This certificate is issued subject to applicable laws, regulations, and conditions as set forth in the instructions portion of this form.

23. DATE ISSUED

24. AUTHORIZED SIGNATURE, ALCOHOL AND TOBACCO TAX AND TRADE BUREAU

FOR TTB USE ONLY

QUALIFICATIONS

EXPIRATION DATE *(If any)*

AFFIX COMPLETE SET OF LABELS BELOW *(See General Instructions 4, 6, and 7)*

TTB F 5100.31 (10/2007)   PREVIOUS EDITIONS ARE OBSOLETE

Notes

Acceptable Changes That May Be Made to Wine Labels that DO NOT Require a New Label Approval

1. When you delete any non-mandatory label information.
2. When you change the shape or proportionate size of the labels.
3. When you change the stated percentages for varietal and or appellation- must total 100%.
4. When you change the net contents to another approved metric standard of fill. 27 CFR 4.37
5. When you change the alcohol content, as long as it remains in the same taxable grade and class/type.
6. When you add, delete or change the state bottle deposit information.
7. When you change the name and/or trade name of responsible winery. NOTE: The name/trade name must appear on the Basic Permit under which the certificate is issued.
8. When you change the stated mandatory amounts of sugar at harvest and/or residual sugar.
9. When you change the stated mandatory caloric content.
10. When you change the name and/or address of the foreign producer, bottler or shipper. NOTE: the producer, bottler or shipper must be located in the same country originally shown.
11. When you change or delete stated vintage date. NOTE: If you DO NOT have a vintage date to begin with, then you must submit a new application if you want to add it.
12. When you add, delete or change the name and/or address or trademark (or both) of the wholesaler, retailer or persons for whom the product is imported or bottled. NOTE: You may add this information by adding another label stating such information provided that no reference is made on the additional label to the product or any of its characteristics.
13. When you change or delete stated bottling date.
14. When you change or delete stated amount of acid and/or ph level.
15. When you add or delete bonded winery number.
16. When you add, delete or change UPC code.
17. When you add, delete, or change a web site address, phone number, fax number or zip code.
18. When you change or delete a lot or batch identification number or other serial numbers.
19. When you add, delete, or change trademark and/or copyright symbols i.e., TM, @ , ®.

THESE CHANGES CAN BE FOUND ON PAGE 3 OF TTB FORM 5100.31

Helpful Hints for Filing Paper COLA applications

- Paper applications must be printed on legal size paper
- Applications must be signed
- Do not make pen or ink changes, or use "white-out," on the labels
- If submitting labels for clear, acetate, etched or painted labels, include a picture of a filled sample bottle
- Include copies of any formulas, pre-import letters or lab analysis results that may pertain to the label
- Include copies of prior approvals (prior to March 10, 2006) for domestic labels using Semi-Generic designations
- Include supporting documentation for Organic labels or labels with biodynamic / agriculture biologique claims
- Make sure labels are completely legible – if we cannot read them, we cannot approve them
- Labels must be affixed to the front of the form. If labels do not fit in the space provided, they may be reduced, but copies must be legible and original size may be attached to application
- Provide translations for any foreign text on labels or on supporting documentation
- Check the list of allowable revisions to approved labels before resubmitting
- We suggest that you do not print your labels prior to receiving label approval
- ***Sign up for COLAs Online!***

Top Ten Reasons for Needing Corrections on Paper COLA Applications
---

1. **Government Warning Statement contains errors**. The Government Warning Statement must appear in type that is at least 1 mm for containers 237 ml or less, 2 mm for containers between 237 ml and 3 L, and at least 3 mm for containers over 3 L in size. The text in the government warning cannot exceed 40 characters per inch for 1 mm type size, 25 characters per inch for 2 mm type size, or 12 characters per inch for 3 mm type size. Separate COLA applications must be submitted for containers that are less than 237 ml, between 237 ml and 3 L, and over 3 L in size. The words "GOVERNMENT WARNING" must appear in capital letters and in bold type. Proofread the government warning for spelling and punctuation errors and missing words prior to submittal.

2. **Appellation of origin problems.** Many issues with the appellation of origin surface, such as: an appellation of origin that is completely missing, when it is required on the label; the appellation is not on the correct label – (it must appear with the class/type designation on the brand label); or the appellation is not officially recognized by the appropriate governing authority; multiple appellations are referenced which do not overlap; or estate bottled wine without a required a viticultural appellation.

3. **Name and address problems.** Trade names must be applied for and approved by the National Revenue Center prior to their use on labels. The company name used on a label in the bottler/importer statement must match exactly with a trade name of record on your permit. The address of the bottler/importer on the label must match what is on the application and permit.

4. **Containers larger than 187 ml require that the sulfit**e statement, the class/type designation, the appellation of origin, the bottler/importer statement, and the net content statement appear in text that is a minimum of 2 mm in size. The alcohol content statement must appear in type that is between 1 and 3 mm for containers 5 L or less in size

5. **Class/Type issues on the label.**

   a) grape varietals appear on the brand label without percentages - If multiple grape varietals appear on the brand label, percentages must be stated in direct conjunction with each varietal, and those percentages must total 100%.
   b) a grape varietal appears in "brand label" text - If a grape varietal appears in brand label text, it must appear separate and apart or be substantially more conspicuous than any surrounding text.
   c) class/type is missing from the label altogether – as a minimum, a generic designation such as "red wine" or "white wine" must be stated on the brand label.
   d) class/type conflicts exist – As an example, the alcohol content places the product in the "table wine" class, but a reference to "dessert wine" appears on the label.

e) the class/type does not appear with the appellation of origin on the brand label, when an appellation is required.

f) An "Other than standard wine" label that is in conflict with the suggested Statement of Composition.

6. **Legibility issues or unacceptable alterations to label copy -** When information on the label is not legible, the application cannot be reviewed. Additionally, labels may not contain pen or ink changes, white out, or paste-over alterations. Label copy submitted with the application must appear in final format, exactly as it will appear on the container.

7. **Alcohol content** The alcohol content appears in the wrong format (alcohol ___% by volume); or alcohol content is the wrong size. Alcohol content must appear in print at least 1 mm and no larger than 3mm in size. The statement of alcohol content must appear on either the brand or strip label.

8. **Misleading statements.** You may not make false or misleading statements on the label. You may not make statements on your label that may create the impression that the wine contains distilled spirits, is comparable to a distilled spirit or has intoxicating qualities.

9. **Items on the application are omitted, or incomplete.** An application is received without a signature from an authorized representative of the company, or additional required information is missing from the application.

10. **The application submitted on outdated forms, or the duplicated copy of the application is submitted in the wrong size.** The new TTB form 5100.31 is available on our website at http://www.ttb.gov/forms/pdfs/5100/f510031.pdf. It must be printed in legal size on legal-sized paper.

Why YOU Should Be Using COLAs Online

1. **Decreased time to obtain a COLA approval**
   - No mailing or courier delays
   - E-applications are processed in half the time as paper applications

2. **Fewer calls to customer service**
   - E-mail confirmation upon submission of application and for subsequent changes in status
   - E-apps offer the ability to track the status of your application throughout the entire process

3. **No outright rejections**
   - If errors are found, during review, labels are returned with "Needs Correction" status
   - This feature offers an opportunity for corrections to be made within 15 calendar days after notice

4. **Corrected e-applications that have been resubmitted receive priority**

5. **The same qualifications that you receive for paper applications are now being used for e-applications**

6. **No rejections for missing data**
   - Eliminate concerns about forgetting your signature or using the wrong form
   - The system will not allow you to submit an incomplete application

7. **Sy stem accessibility**
   - Submissions can be made 7 days a week, 23 hours a day
   - The system can be accessed from any PC with an internet connection and Microsoft IE

8. **Facilitates Record Keeping**
   - A record of all approved COLAs
   - Copies of approved COLAs can be printed from the system

Helpful Hints for Preventing Image Problems with COLAs Online

1. Only Jpeg (.jpg) or Tiff (.tif) files may be used for label images.

2. Document files (.pdf and .doc) may ONLY be uploaded under Attachments, along with .jpg and .tif files.

3. The maximum file size the system permits is 450 kb for each individual file being uploaded as a label or attachment.

4. High compression settings of the image will file cause labels to be blurry, or too small to read. Set the compression ratio to MEDIUM or LOW so the file size is close to but within file size limit of 450KB. A file size of less than 100 KB is an indication that the compression may be too high.

5. If a images appear as a Red X, the wrong color mode was used on image files. The system only accepts label images with the type/extensions of .jpg or .tif format utilizing the RGB color mode/space. Images in the CMYK color mode/space are unacceptable in COLAs Online.

6. If the label image bears a "color bar" or other distortion, the resolution may not be correct. We recommend that the resolution rate be set at 150 DPI (Dots Per Inch) or within the range of 120 DPI to 200 DPI.

7. The label file must contain only the label and must be cropped of all surrounding white space or other text.

   - All outside measurements that are not a part of the actual label must be removed before upload.

   - All printer's proof information surrounding label copy must be removed.

   - The dimensions entered when uploading the labels take into account the entire file, including both the label image and any surrounding white space or text.

   - Exact measurements of the printed label which will appear on the container must be used.

   When reviewing images from the "view Eapp" screen, place the cursor to the right of the image (but not on the image), and right click the mouse. Then click on "Select All" and this will highlight the image, including any "white space" around the image.

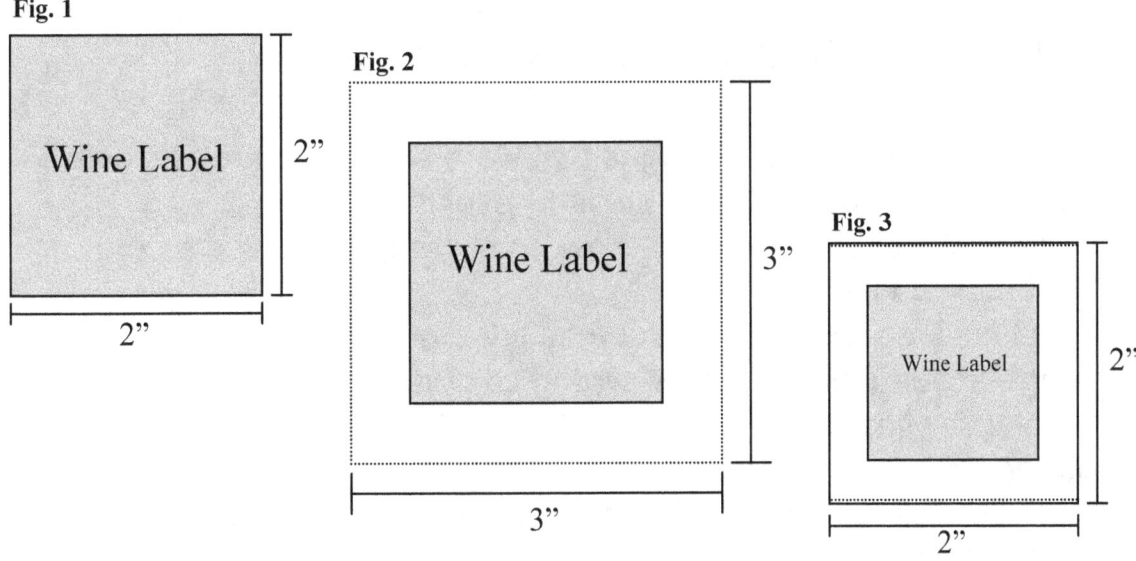

Fig. 1 - Actual size of the label   Fig. 2 - Actual size of image uploaded   Fig. 3 - Image result

Other image issues:

- Ensure that label dimensions are entered correctly. Remember that the dimensions requested when uploading a label image pertain to the entire file.
- Each label must be uploaded separately and identified as "Brand", "Back", "Strip", "Neck" or "Other".
- A separate application must be submitted for each product.
- Make sure your images are legible - IF YOU CAN'T READ IT, WE CAN'T READ IT!

Avoid submitting applications with image problems by verifying your images.
Click on the file name in Step 3 of the application to view the uploaded image.

Resubmitting Corrected Image Files

If your application is returned for correction, make the necessary corrections to your image file. Then open the application and go to Step 3.

- Remove the original image
- Find and upload the new image
- Choose the type of label you are uploading
- Enter the dimensions of the label
- Click on "Attach file"

Top Ten Errors
for COLAs Online Applications

- High compression - the images that were submitted are not legible
- Image was distorted during upload (resolution error)
- Dimensions used generate a skewed or distorted image on the Printable version of the COLA
- Labels not saved and uploaded as separate image files
- Image appears as a Red X – wrong color mode used
- Problems with the Government Warning (Health Warning Statement)
- Terms placed in incorrect fields... i.e. "zinfandel" in the fanciful name section
- Alcohol content and vintage date on labels do not match application
- Trade name appearing in the bottler's statement on labels does not match the application
- Brand name on e-app does not match the label

These are examples of reasons why we would return an application with the status of "Needs Correction."

The "Needs Correction" offers the benefit of immediate notification of any corrections that are required. In addition to this feature, the application also receives priority upon resubmission.

OMB No. 1513-0111 (3/31/2009)

ALFD TRACKING NUMBER

DEPARTMENT OF THE TREASURY
ALCOHOL AND TOBACCO TAX AND TRADE BUREAU (TTB)
COLAs ONLINE ACCESS REQUEST

Submit this form to the Advertising, Labeling and Formulation Division, TTB, 1310 G Street, N.W., Suite 400E, Washington, DC 20220

A – ACTION REQUESTED - Please read instructions to check appropriate box

1.
☐ NEW USER   ☐ PREPARER/REVIEWER   ☐ MODIFY USER/ ADD PERMIT   ☐ DELETE USER   ☐ REACTIVATE USER

2. IF MODIFYING, DELETING, OR REACTIVATING THEN PROVIDE EXISTING USER ID, *if known*

B – USER INFORMATION: *Please complete section B with all the required data to establish a user identification record.*

3. FIRST NAME	4. MIDDLE INITIAL	5. LAST NAME	6. SUFFIX *(i.e., Jr., Sr., III)*
7. LABEL REP ID NUMBER, if any	8. DATE OF BIRTH	9. MOTHER'S MAIDEN NAME	10. EMPLOYEE TITLE
11. BUSINESS PHONE NUMBER	12. BUSINESS E-MAIL ADDRESS (required)		
13. BUSINESS FAX NUMBER	14. BUSINESS MAILING ADDRESS OF PERSON REQUESTING ACCESS TO COLAs ONLINE *(if different than 15.)*		

C – COMPANY INFORMATION: *Provide information about the company for which you request to e-file applications*

15. NAME AND STREET ADDRESS OF COMPANY AS IT APPEARS ON THE REGISTRY, PERMIT, OR BREWER'S NOTICE

16. REGISTRY, PERMIT, OR BREWER'S NOTICE NUMBER(S) FOR THE ABOVE ADDRESS *(Use a separate sheet if necessary. See instructions.)*

REQUESTOR'S CERTIFICATION

I hereby attest that the entries on this form are true and correct, and that the unique username and password, or digital signature that the Alcohol and Tobacco Tax and Trade Bureau assigned to me are intended as my original signature. I intend that such submissions be treated as bearing an original signature for all intents and purposes when submitting applications electronically via COLAs Online system.

17. REQUESTOR'S SIGNATURE	18. DATE

D – APPROVAL REQUIRED: *Signature of the company official with signature authority required to grant access to COLAs Online.*

19. COMPANY APPROVAL SIGNATURE	20. PRINT NAME AND TITLE OF COMPANY APPROVAL OFFICIAL	21. DATE

FOR TTB USE ONLY

	DATE	COMMENTS
USER VERIFICATION COMPLETED		
SYSTEM OWNER APPROVAL		
TTB OPERATIONS COMPLETED		
SYSTEM ADMINISTRATOR COMPLETED		
USER NOTIFICATION COMPLETED		

TTB F 5013.2 (02/2008)

INSTRUCTIONS

You must complete this form in order to receive a User ID and password to obtain access to TTB's COLAs Online System. Each user must obtain an individual User ID and password which is not to be shared with anyone. Sharing your User ID and password can result in cancellation of your COLAs Online privileges.

Section A – You must check the appropriate box:

(1) Check *New User* for full access to COLAs Online if you have not been previously supplied with a User ID and password. Persons with wholesalers permits can only apply if relabeling.

(2) Check *Preparer/Reviewer* for limited access to COLAs Online (This access is used only for preparing/reviewing electronic applications).

(3) Check *Modify User/Add Permit* only if you already have a User ID and password to COLAs Online. You must also complete the remainder of the form as instructed below to include all modifications and include your previous User ID.

(4) Check *Delete User* if you no longer want access to COLAs Online for yourself or another user. Please provide the User ID of the user to be deleted, if known (Section A, Item 2).

(5) Check *Reactivate User* if we cancelled your original User ID due to inactivity and you wish to begin using the COLAs Online system again. You must also complete the remainder of the form as instructed below and include your previous User ID.

Section B - You must enter the required information about the individual requesting access to COLAs Online in items 3 - 14. Item 11 should only be completed by third party filers (e.g. trade associations, law firms, consultants). Third party filers who have not previously been assigned a Rep ID number must request one from ALFD at 1-866-927-2533, before submitting this form.

Section C - You must enter the required information about the company for which you are requesting to file applications. This information must appear exactly as it does on the Plant Registry, Basic Permit, or Brewer's Notice. Be sure to enter the correct number in item 16 (example: BW-PA-00, PA-I-00, DSP-PA-00, BR-PA-AAA). If you are filing for multiple Registry/Permit/Brewer's Notice Numbers, you may include a list of them on a separate sheet attached to this form. The attached list must include the company name and address, Registry, Permit or Brewer's Notice Number, and approval signature by a company official with signing authority for each permit for which you are requesting access. Any person without signature authority must also attach a separate TTB F 5000.8, Power of Attorney, for each company on behalf of which they will be filing label applications.

Section D - A company official with TTB signing authority must sign, print his or her name and title, and date the form in items 19-21.

You must send the original of this form to:

> Advertising, Labeling and Formulation Division (ALFD)
> Alcohol and Tobacco Tax and Trade Bureau
> 1310 G Street, N.W.
> Suite 400E
> Washington, DC 20220

Your User ID will be sent to you via e-mail and your password will be provided separately via telephone for security reasons.

PRIVACY ACT INFORMATION

We provide this information to comply with Section 3 of the Privacy Act of 1974 (5 U.S.C. 552a(e)(3)).

We require this information under the authority of 27 U.S.C. 205(e). You must disclose this information so we can identify the company on whose behalf the applicant claims to act, to verify the scope of the applicant's authority to act, and to evaluate the applicant's qualifications for access to the system.

We use this information to approve, grant, and control access to sensitive information systems. In addition, the information may be disclosed to other Federal, State, and local law enforcement and regulatory agency personnel to verify information on the application and to aid in the performance of their duties. The information may further be disclosed to the Justice Department if it appears that the furnishing of false information may contribute to a violation of Federal law. Disclosure may otherwise be made pursuant to the routine uses most recently published in the Federal Registry for ATF's Regulatory Enforcement Records System (Treasury/ATF.008).

If you fail to supply complete information then there will be a delay in the processing of your application.

PAPERWORK REDUCTION ACT NOTICE

This request is in accordance with the Paperwork Reduction Act of 1995. We use this information to authenticate end users in the program to electronically file Certificates of Label Approval. The information is used by the Government to verify the identity of the end users prior to issuing them passwords. The information we request is voluntary, however, if the requested information is not submitted, the users will not be granted a password and cannot participate in the electronic filing program.

The estimated average burden associated with this collection is 19 minutes per respondent or recordkeeper depending on the individual circumstances. Comments concerning the accuracy of this burden estimate and suggestions for reducing this burden should be directed to the Reports Management Officer, Regulations and Rulings Division, Alcohol and Tobacco Tax and Trade Bureau, Washington, DC 20220.

An agency may not conduct or sponsor, and a person is not required to respond to, a collection of information unless it displays a current, valid OMB control number.

TTB F 5013.2 (02/2008)

OMB No. 1513-0014 (10/31/09)

DEPARTMENT OF THE TREASURY
ALCOHOL AND TOBACCO TAX AND TRADE BUREAU (TTB)

POWER OF ATTORNEY

(Please read instructions before completing this form)

1. PRINCIPAL *(Name of Partnership, Corporation, Association, Estate, or Individual)*	2. BUSINESS IN WHICH ENGAGED

3. ADDRESS *(Number, Street, City, State, ZIP Code), TELEPHONE NUMBER AND E-MAIL ADDRESS*

4. TAXPAYER IDENTIFICATION NUMBER *(Employer Identification Number or Social Security Number)*	5. PERMIT NUMBER / REGISTRY NUMBER *(If applicable)*

6. NAME AND TELEPHONE NUMBER OF APPOINTED ATTORNEY

7. ADDRESS *(Number, Street, City, State, and ZIP Code)*

8. The above named principal, engaged in the business shown, has appointed the above named attorney to: *(See Instruction 2)*

(a) Execute for him/her all applications, notices, bonds, tax returns, tax information disclosure authorizations, and other instruments, claims, offers in compromise, letters, writings, and papers, and to act for him/her in dealing with the Alcohol and Tobacco Tax and Trade Bureau (TTB) in connection with matters relating to the laws and regulations administered by it. The principal authorizes the attorney named above to receive on his/her behalf any and all notices, papers, and letters from the Alcohol and Tobacco Tax and Trade Bureau in connection with all such matters, and grants him/her full power and authority to do all that is essential in and about the premises, as duly as the principal could do if personally present, with full power of substitution and revocation. The principal hereby ratifies and confirms all that the attorney must lawfully do or cause to be by virtue of this appointment.

(b)

9. The power is to apply to the following. *(If authority is restricted to a particular factory, plant, premises, etc., give name as: Distilled Spirits Plant, Tobacco Products Factory, Tobacco Export Warehouse, etc., and address and registry number; or, if a Wholesale Liquor Dealer, SDA, or Tax-Free Alcohol User; or if this Power of Attorney may be used for manufacturing or importing firearms or ammunition, etc., give permit number.)*

10. SIGNATURE OF APPOINTED ATTORNEY

EXECUTION *(See Instruction 3)*		
11. SIGNATURE IF PRINCIPAL IS INDIVIDUAL *(Signature of Principal)*		DATE

12. SIGNATURE IF PRINCIPAL IS PARTNERSHIP, LIMITED LIABILITY PARTNERSHIP (LLP), ESTATE, CORPORATION, LIMITED LIABILITY COMPANY (LLC), OR ASSOCIATION. Under penalties of perjury, I declare that I have the authority to execute this power of attorney on behalf of the principal			13. Seal of Corporation, Association, or LLC (A corporation, association or LLC will impress their seal below if they have one. If there is no seal, provide a resolution by the board of directors or organizational/supporting documents that support your company not having a seal, if applicable)
Signature	Title	Date	
Signature	Title	Date	
Signature	Title	Date	
Signature	Title	Date	

TTB F 5000.8 (11/2006)

Page 1 of 2

14. ACKNOWLEDGMENT, WITNESSING, OR DECLARATION (Complete 14a, 14b, or 14c)

14a. ACKNOWLEDGMENT	14b. WITNESSING
The above-named person(s) signing as or for the principal(s) appeared before me today and acknowledged this power of attorney as his/her/their voluntary act and deed. The notarial seal must be affixed unless a seal is not required under the laws of the state where the power of attorney is executed.	This power of attorney was signed by or for the principal(s) by a person or persons known to, and in the presence of, the two disinterested witnesses whose signatures appear below:

NOTARIAL SEAL (If required)	Signature of Notary or Other Officer	Signature of Witness	Date
	Date Title	Signature of Witness	Date

14c. DECLARATION by attorney, certified public accountant, or enrolled practitioner who is granted the power of attorney by this form

I declare that I am aware of the regulations of 31 CFR Part 8, that I am not currently under suspension or disbarment from practice before the Alcohol and Tobacco Tax and Trade Bureau, and that I am currently: *(Check applicable box)*

☐ A member in good standing of the bar of the highest court of¹ _____

☐ Qualified to practice as a certified public accountant in¹ _____

Printed Name _____

¹Insert Name of State, Possession, or District of Columbia

Signature _____

FOR TTB USE ONLY

DATE RECEIVED FOR FILING	DISTRICT	RECEIVED BY *(Signature and Title)*
DATE RECEIVED FOR FILING	TTB OFFICE	RECEIVED BY *(Signature and Title)*

INSTRUCTIONS

1. GENERAL. This form is filed with each TTB office in which the appointed attorney is to represent the principal.

2. ITEM 8. A full power of attorney is granted by paragraph 8(a). The power of attorney may be limited or restricted by deleting all of paragraph 8(a) and listing the specific powers to be conferred in section 8(b).

3. EXECUTION. This form must be signed by or on behalf of the principal(s) as follows:

   (a) INDIVIDUAL by his or her completion of item 11.

   (b) PARTNERSHIP, LIMITED LIABILITY PARTNERSHIP (LLP) by completion of item 12 by all partners, or one partner who attaches his/her authorization to act on behalf of all the partners unless this authorization is provided by State law.

   (c) CORPORATION or ASSOCIATION by completion of items 12 and 13, an officer, preferably the president, vice-president, or treasurer, must sign in item 12.

   (d) ESTATE by completion of item 12 by the executor or administrator and attaching other such documents as may be required by TTB.

   (e) LIMITED LIABILITY COMPANY (LLC) by completion of item 12 by all members or managers, or one member or manager who attaches his/her authorization to act on behalf of the LLC.

4. FILING. This form must be completed in duplicate, unless otherwise required, and submitted to the Director, National Revenue Center, 550 Main St, Ste. 8002, Cincinnati, OH 45202-5215. The original with any attachments will be retained by the Director, National Revenue Center, and all other copies will be returned to the principal. If the power of attorney is applicable to more than one business establishment, additional copies must be submitted for each.

The additional copies will be filed in the same manner as when the power of attorney relates to only one establishment or business. Copies reproduced by photographic process need not be certified as copies of the original.

5. ORIGINAL OF A RULING. The Alcohol and Tobacco Tax and Trade Bureau will give to an appointed attorney the original of a ruling concerning the principal about TTB matters if a statement is made to that effect in item 8(b).

6. REVOCATION. A power of attorney remains in effect until revoked by the principal in written notice to the Director, National Revenue Center.

7. RULES. All persons representing clients before the Alcohol and Tobacco Tax and Trade Bureau must comply with the regulations governing representation *(26 CFR Part 601 or those regulations as recodified in 27 CFR Part 71)* and any other applicable rules and statutes.

PAPERWORK REDUCTION ACT NOTICE

This request is in accordance with the Paperwork Reduction Act of 1995. The information collection is used by TTB to ensure that only duly authorized individuals are signing documents. The information is voluntary.

The estimated average burden associated with this collection of information is 30 minutes per respondent or recordkeeper, depending on individual circumstances. Comments concerning the accuracy of this burden estimate and suggestions for reducing this burden should be addressed to the Reports Management Officer, Regulations and Rulings Division, Alcohol and Tobacco Tax and Trade Bureau, Washington, DC 20220.

An agency may not conduct or sponsor, and a person is not required to respond to, a collection of information unless it displays a current, valid OMB control number.

Page 2 of 2

TTB F 5000.8 (11/2006)

Advertising, Labeling & Formulation Division

Main number/Customer Service: 202-453-2243 or 1-866-927-2533

Option 1 - Address, fax number and hours
Option 2 - COLAs Online technical assistance
Option 3 - COLAs Online registration assistance
Option 4 - Formulation, Malt Beverage and Distilled Spirits
Option 5 - Advertising / Market Compliance Office
Option 6 - Wine Labeling

Email: alfd@ttb.gov

ALFD
1310 G Street, N.W.
Suite 400-E
Washington, DC 20220

Karen   Freelove, Director   202-453-2139

Teresa Knapp, Assistant Director   202-453-2108
Wine   Labeling Office   202-453-2984   (fax)

Gracie Joy, Assistant Director   202-453-2044
Formulation, Malt Beverage &   202-453-2982 (fax)
Distilled Spirit Labeling Office

Susan Berndt, Assistant Director   202-453-2153
Market   Compliance Office   202-453-2985   (fax)

Donna   Smith   202-453-2146
Supervisor   y,   202-453-2983   (fax)
Information   Technology

COLAs   Online Registrations   202-453-2983(fax)

www.ttb.gov provides forms, regulations and frequently asked questions

Bottled or Packed Wine Record
27 CFR 24.308

A proprietor who bottles, packs or receives bottled or packed beverage wine in bond must maintain a record by tax class. The parts of 27 CFR 24.308 that usually pertain to bonded winery operations require that the following information be recorded:

☐ The date of the transaction

☐ The tax class, kind of wine, number and size of bottle filled

☐ The volume of wine bottled

☐ The volume of bottled wine received in bond, transferred in bond, taxpaid, dumped to bulk, used for tasting and testing

☐ The quantity recorded as breakage

☐ The label used on bottles or other containers will be shown by using the "Applicant's Serial No." which appears on Item 2 of the label approval Form 5100.31 or a similar system which will allow for verification of labels used on containers

☐ The fill and alcohol tests required by 27 CFR 24.255 *(See next page...)*

☐ Records have sufficient detail to justify tax credit for Small Producers under the provisions of 26 U.S.C. 5041(c)

Bottling or Packing Wine
27 CFR 24.255

(a) General. Proprietors of a bonded wine premises and a taxpaid wine bottling house premises shall be held strictly responsible for the correct determination of the quantity and alcohol content of wine removed. As required by Sec. 24.170, appropriate and accurate measures and instruments for measuring and testing the wine will be provided at each wine premises.

(b) Bottle or other container fill. Proprietors of bonded wine premises and taxpaid wine bottling house premises shall fill bottles or other containers as nearly as possible to conform to the amount shown on the label or blown in the bottle or marked on any container other than a bottle;

but in no event may the amount of wine contained in any individual bottle, due to lack of uniformity of the bottles, vary from the amount stated more than 1.0 percent for 15.0 liters and above, 1.5 percent for 1.0 liter to 14.9 liters, 2.0 percent for 750 mL, 3.0 percent for 375 mL, 4.5 percent for 187 mL and 100 mL, and 9.0 percent for 50 mL;

and in such case, there will be substantially as many bottles overfilled as there are bottles underfilled for each lot of wine bottled. Short-filled bottles or other containers of wine which are sold or otherwise disposed of by the proprietor to employees for personal consumption need not be labeled, but, if labeled, need not show an accurate statement of net contents.

(c) Tax tolerance. The net contents of bottles or other containers of untaxpaid wine in the same tax class filled during six consecutive tax return periods, as determined from the bonded wine premises proprietor's fill test records, shall not vary by more than 0.5 percent from the net contents as stated on the bottles or other containers. The bonded wine premises proprietor is liable for the tax on the entire amount of wine in the same tax class when that wine is removed from bond, without benefit of tolerance, when the fill of bottles or other containers exceeds a 0.5 percent average of a period which consists of six consecutive tax returns, or when filling is not conducted in compliance with good commercial practice.

(d) Fill tests. The proprietor shall test at representative intervals wine bottled or packed during the bottling or packing operation of each bottling or packing line to determine if the wine contained in the bottle or other container is in agreement with that stated on the label, bottle, or other container.

(e) Alcohol tests. The proprietor shall test the alcohol content by volume to determine the tax class of the wine and to ensure the alcohol content to be stated on the label is in agreement with the requirement of Sec. 24.257.

This is an example of a Bottling Form that has all of the information required for the Bottled or Packed Wine Record:

Bottling Form

Vintage: 2004	Variety: Zinfandel	Date: 3/24/2006

Bottles

Company	CalGlass	LW

Shape	Color	Size
___ Special Burgundy (Prestige)	✓ Champagne Green	___ 375 ml
___ Burgundy Push Up	___ Dead Leaf Green	✓ 750 ml
✓ Bordeaux (Claret)	___ Flint	___ 1.5 ml
___ Hock	___ Amber	___ 3 liter
___ Burgundy Flat	___ Other	___ 5 liter
___ Other		___ 6 liter
		___ Other

Bottles Per Case: ___ 6   ✓ 12   Cases Per Pallet: 56

Labeled: Y ✓   N ___
If no, when: _____

UPC Code: 7540300030

Label Bottling Code: COLA #06-12

Low SO2   Pallet #s   all
High SO2   Pallet #s   _____

Corks (Logo 9 x 1/3/4)

Company Name	Grade	Pallet #s
Porto Cork	Extra First	all

Foils (Logo)

Grade	Color
✓ Tin	___ Black
___ Polylam	✓ Gold

Tank: 215

Beginning Number of Gallons: 3998	Number of Cases Produced: 1679
Number of Gallons Used: 3998	Gallon Equivalent: 3991.9
Number of Gallons Remaining: 0	Gain/(Loss) During Bottling: (6.1)

Wine moved to:

Location	Number of Cases	Number of Bottles
A-3	1679	0

Fill level			Analysis	
6.00	750 ml	58F	pH	3.45
9.15	751 ml	58F	TA	6.9
7.12	750 ml	59 F	RS	dry
14.45	749 ml	59 F	Alc	14.3
17.00	751 ml	59F		

Memo:

~Sample Record~

Signature: Roger Jones   Date: 3/24/2006
(Individual counting inventory)

TTB Wine FAQ #8: What are the rules for transfer of unlabeled bottled wine?

🖱 http://www.ttb.gov/wine/faq.shtml#w8

TTB has received inquires about the transfer, labeling, recordkeeping and taxpayment of unlabeled bottled wine (sometimes called "shiners").

When unlabeled bottled wine is transferred among two or more bonded wine premises for aging or labeling, the bottler must provide a copy of the approved Application For And Certification/Exemption of Label/Bottle Approval (COLA) TTB Form 5100.31 under which the wine was bottled. The transfer in bond record which accompanies the wine must be accurate and specific, and the label information record for the wine must fully support any claims made on the label to be affixed to the wine.

The responsibility for transferring accurate label information is not that of the producer alone; it is the responsibility of all holders of the wine from the time it is produced until it is removed from bond for consumption or sale.
Here are guidelines for the various parties that may be involved when unlabeled bottled wine is transferred among bonded premises:

What are the responsibilities of the Producer? The producer of the wine must ensure that the transfer in bond record required by 27 CFR 24.309 contains accurate and specific label information for all bulk wine shipped in bond (or taxpaid) to another premises for bottling. This allows the bottler to apply for a COLA and ensures that the product label is correct.

What are the responsibilities of the Bottler? The bottler obtains a COLA which can be substantiated by the transfer record which accompanied the wine from the producer. Unless the wine will be bottled at a taxpaid wine bottling house, the bottler will make sure that the wine to be bottled is received and maintained on bonded (not taxpaid) premises. The bottler maintains records in accordance with 27 CFR 24.308.

If the bottler transfers unlabeled bottled wine to another bonded premises for labeling, the bottler must send the wine in bond (untaxpaid) with the COLA under which the wine was bottled. If a different product label will be affixed, the bottler must obtain a correct COLA, and forward it to the premises where the label will be affixed. The transfer in bond record that accompanies the bottled wine must contain accurate and specific information which substantiates the product label, as specified by 27 CFR 24.309. However, if unlabeled bottled wine is transferred to another bonded premises for aging only, and will be subsequently returned to the bottler for the affixing of the product label, the COLA does not have to accompany the shipments.

To reiterate, an approved label which accompanies the wine must carry the minimum label requirements, but it might not be the label eventually affixed to the product. The label used to bottle the wine is sometimes referred to as the "generic" label. The bottler may apply for another COLA for a product label with specific label claims, as long as the claims are substantiated by the label information record requirements of 27 CFR 24.314.

What does the Labeler receive from the Bottler? The person who will affix the product label receives the unlabeled, untaxpaid bottled wine, the COLA for the product label to be affixed, and the transfer in bond record (27 CFR 24.309) which contains accurate and specific information which substantiates the label claims.

Only the bottler of the wine may apply for a COLA. If the owner of unlabeled bottled wine wants to label the wine with a label other than that which accompanied the wine, the bottler must be contacted, and the bottler must work with the owner to obtain an approved product label which is fully substantiated by the label information record for that wine.

What if the bottler is unable to provide a COLA? If the bottler of the wine is unable to obtain label approval for the wine to be labeled, the wine may only be labeled if it is dumped to bulk and re-bottled. It may be re-bottled when an appropriate COLA is obtained by the bottler. The label may not contain any information which is not fully supported by the label information record for the wine.

What is the responsibility of the person who removes the wine from bond? If the labeled wine is transferred in bond to another bonded wine premises for taxable removal, it must be accompanied by the transfer in bond record (27 CFR 24.309) which contains accurate and specific information which substantiates the label claims.

The person who pays the tax on the wine is the qualified proprietor of a bonded winery or bonded wine cellar, and not a wholesaler, wine broker, agent, negotiant, retailer, consumer or, necessarily, the actual owner of the wine. Bottled wine may not be removed from bond (i.e., tax paid) without a COLA and an approved product label being affixed.

How long must the records be kept? All records must be retained for a period of not less than three years from the record date or the date of last entry required to be made in the record, whichever is later. However, TTB may require records to be kept for a period of not more than three additional years, if deemed necessary.

# # #

Wine FAQ #14: May I use a winemaking kit for commercial wine production?

🖱http://www.ttb.gov/wine/faq.shtml#w14

Does TTB regulate the production of home winemaking kits?

No, we do not. Winemaking kits typically contain concentrate, yeast, juice, acids, sulfites and wood chips, and provide sufficient materials to produce about 30 bottles of wine. Since the kits contain unfermented raw materials, they do not come under our jurisdiction. When the kits are used to produce tax-exempt wine for personal or family use, we do not regulate the labeling of wine made from the kits.

Does TTB endorse or certify the contents of winemaking kits?

No, TTB does not endorse or certify the contents of any winemaking kits. The users of winemaking kits are fully responsible for obtaining the necessary information about the content of the kits to support any statements made on the label.

What rules apply if I use a winemaking kit to produce wine for sale?

TTB regulates the commercial production of wine under the Internal Revenue Code of 1986 (IRC) and the Federal Alcohol Administration (FAA) Act laws and regulations. These laws and regulations require that wine producers qualify their premises as a bonded wine cellar, obtain an FAA Act basic permit as a producer of wine, pay the applicable excise tax on wine between one-half of 1 percent to 24 percent of alcohol by volume, and receive a Certificate of Label Approval (COLA) for all wine that is bottled.

The IRC and FAA Act requirements apply to those who are engaged in the business of winemaking who intend to sell the wine or distribute it for commercial purposes, and apply equally to companies using kits and traditional winemaking materials. Information provided on the labels of all wine made for commercial purposes must be truthful and must adequately inform the consumer about the identity and quality of the product.

How should I label wine made with a kit?

If you are selling the wine, you must comply with TTB's wine labeling regulations in 27 CFR Part 4 and the Health Warning Statement regulations found in 27 CFR Part 16, as well as any applicable State regulations.

In addition to the mandatory label statements required by Part 4, TTB must be able to verify any optional statements used on wine labels. Examples of optional label claims include the varietal content (type of grape or grapes used), the appellation of origin (the geographic origin of the winemaking materials), and the vintage date (year of harvest). Winemakers using kits who wish to show any optional claims on the label must obtain appropriate records from the kit's producer to verify the contents, the origin of the winemaking materials, the vintage date, etc.

When winemakers make optional claims on wine, additional regulatory requirements in 27 CFR Part 4 are triggered, beyond the requirement to document the claims. For example, if 75 percent of the grapes used in a wine are from a particular State, the wine must be fully finished in that State or an adjacent State in order to be entitled to use the name of the State as an appellation of origin (27 CFR 4.25). If you buy a kit with 75 percent Washington State concentrate, but produce wine from the kit in Indiana, the wine is not entitled to a Washington State appellation of origin. With proper documentation, you could use "American" as the appellation of origin. Wine with an "American" appellation is not entitled to show a vintage date. Under 27 CFR 4.27, vintage dated wine must have an appellation of origin smaller than a country, and the records must show that 85 percent of the wine is derived from grapes harvested within the given year (95 percent for viticultural areas).

How should I label the wine if I cannot obtain information about the origin of the concentrate or if the wine does not meet the requirements for optional claims?

If information about the origin of the concentrate cannot be verified, the product may be labeled as "grape wine" or with a color descriptor, such as "red wine" or "white wine." If the wine has an alcohol content that is not over 14 percent alcohol by volume, it may also be designated as "table wine."

Vintage dates, varietal names and appellations may not be shown on the label, unless they can be verified and the wine meets the other requirements in 27 CFR part 4 for use of the claim.

If I am selling the wine, may I use the wine treating materials that are often provided in winemaking kits?

You may, if the wine treating materials included in kits are listed as authorized for use and used as shown in the TTB regulations at 27 CFR § 24.246.

#

Label Information Record
27 CFR 24.314

"A proprietor who removes bottled or packed wine with information stated on the label (e.g., varietal, vintage, and appellation of origin, analytical data, and date of harvest) shall have complete records so that the information appearing on the label may be verified by an *[sic]* TTB audit. A wine is not entitled to have information stated on the label unless the information can be readily verified by a complete and accurate record trail from the beginning source material to removal of the wine for consumption or sale. All records necessary to verify wine label information are subject to the record retention requirements of 27 CFR 24.300(d)."

Examples of such records may include:

Receipt Records

1. Date of Transaction
2. Origin of the grapes, i.e., from whom purchased and location of the vineyard
3. Weight certificates or similar receipt documents
4. Grower or field tags and trucking documents
5. Quantity of grapes or wine received
6. Chemistry of grapes (Brix, acidity, pH, alcohol)
7. Documentation for any other label claim desired, such as age of vines, dry farmed, etc.

Crush Records

1. If claimed, varietal, vintage, appellation of origin percentages
2. Transaction date
3. Tank into which grapes are crushed
4. Movements between tanks, such as drain and pressing operations

Fermentation Records

1. If claimed, varietal, vintage, appellation of origin percentages
2. Crush tank(s) from which received
3. Documentation of movements between fermenters
4. Quantity removed from fermenter after completion of fermentation (produced wine)

Storage Records

1. Transaction date
2. If claimed, varietal, vintage, appellation of origin percentages
3. Quantity and from where received, such as from a fermenting tank, storage tank, or in the case of receipts in bond, the transfer document(s)
4. Percentages of varietal, etc., must be recalculated after blending, including topping
5. Other dispositions such as transfers in bond, taxable removals, bottling, etc.

Petitioning for Approval of a New Grape Variety
27 CFR 4.93

Any interested person may petition the Director for the approval of a grape variety name. The petition may be in the form of a letter and should provide evidence of the following:

1. Acceptance of the new grape variety,
2. The validity of the name for identifying the grape variety,
3. That the variety is used or will be used in winemaking, and
4. That the variety is grown and used in the United States.

Documentation submitted with the petition to establish these items may include reference to the publication of the name of the variety in a scientific or professional journal of horticulture or a published report by a professional, scientific or winegrowers' organization, reference to a plant patent, if so patented, and Information pertaining to the commercial potential of the variety, such as the acreage planted and its location or market studies.

A grape variety name will not be approved if the name has previously been used for a different grape variety, or if the name contains a term or name found to be misleading under Sec. 4.39, or if the name of a new grape variety contains the term "Riesling."

For new grape varieties developed in the United States, TTB may determine if the use of names which contain words of geographical significance, place names, or foreign words are misleading under Sec. 4.39. A grape variety name found to be misleading will not be approved.

#

Petitioning to Establish a New American Viticultural Area
27 CFR 9.3

A written petition may be sent to TTB to establish a new American Viticultural Area. The petition must contain the following information:

1. Evidence that the name of the viticultural area is locally and/or nationally known as referring to the area specified in the application;

2. Historical or current evidence that the boundaries of the viticultural area are as specified in the application;

3. Evidence relating to the geographical features (climate, soil, elevation, physical features, etc.) which distinguish the viticultural features of the proposed area from surrounding areas;

4. The specific boundaries of the viticultural area, based on features which can be found on United States Geological Survey (U.S.G.S.) maps of the largest applicable scale; and

5. A copy of the appropriate U.S.G.S. map(s) with the boundaries prominently marked. (For U.S.G.S. maps, write the U.S. Geological Survey, Branch of Distribution, Box 25286, Federal Center, Denver, Colorado 80225. If the map name is not known, request a map index by State.)

Notes

Recordkeeping Matters

Time of making entries: At the time the operation or transaction occurs, or, if posted from source records, no later than the close of business of the third business day following the day the operation or transaction occurs. 27 CFR 24.300(b)

Record retention: Returns, reports and records, including source records, must be kept for three years from the record date or the date of the last entry required to be made in the record, whichever is later. 27 CFR 24.300(d)

Data Processing: Data maintained on data processing equipment may be kept at the wine premises or at another location, if the original operation or transaction source records are kept available for inspection at the wine premises. 27 CFR 24.300(e)

Photographic copies of records: Reproduced records may be treated as original documents for examination. 27 CFR 24.300(f)

Application File: A complete and current application file must be maintained, readily available at the wine premises for inspection. 27 CFR 24.117 and 27 CFR 24.109

Part 24, Subpart O – Records and Reports

24.300 General.
24.301 Bulk still wine record.
24.302 Effervescent wine record.
24.303 Formula wine record.
24.304 Chaptalization (Brix adjustment) and amelioration record.
24.305 Sweetening record.
24.306 Distilling material or vinegar stock record.
24.307 Nonbeverage wine record.
24.308 Bottled or packed wine record.
24.309 Transfer in bond record.
24.310 Taxpaid removals from bond record.
24.311 Taxpaid wine records.
24.312 Unmerchantable wine returned to bond record.
24.313 Inventory record.
24.314 Label information record.
24.315 Materials received and used record.
24.316 Spirits record.
24.317 Sugar record.
24.318 Acid record.
24.319 Carbon dioxide record.
24.320 Chemical record.
24.321 Decolorizing material record.
24.322 Allied products record.
24.323 Excise Tax Return form.

136

In addition to the records previously discussed, here is information about other records which may need to be maintained, depending upon the operations conducted at your bonded wine premises:

Materials Received and Used Record
27 CFR 24.315

Wine producers must maintain a record showing the receipt and use of basic winemaking materials on wine premises. The record must contain the following information:
- Date of receipt
- Quantity received
- Name and address from whom received
- Date of use or other disposition

(See 27 CFR 24.246 for list of materials authorized for treatment of wine and juice.)

Acid Record
27 CFR 24.318

If acid is used on wine premises, a record containing the information listed below must be maintained. The Acid Record may be a compilation of source documents OR a summary record.
- Date of use
- Kind and quantity of acid used
- Kinds and volume of juice or wine in which used
- When used to correct natural deficiency, the fixed acid level of juice or wine before and after the addition of acid

Sugar Record
27 CFR 24.317

A proprietor who receives, stores, or uses sugar must maintain a record of receipt and use. Invoices covering purchases must be retained. The record must show the following:
- Date of receipt and from whom received
- Kind and quantity
- Amount used for production of allied products
- Amount removed from the wine premises

When used for chaptalization, amelioration or sweetening, record must show the date, kind and quantity used.

Chemical Record
27 CFR 24.320

A record of the receipt and use of any chemicals must be maintained which contains the information listed below. The Chemical Record may be a compilation of source documents OR a summary record.

- • Receipt:
- • Kinds and quantities received
- • Date of receipt
- • Names and addresses from whom purchased

Use in Juice or Wine: (Except for filtering aids, inert fining agents, sulfur dioxide, carbon dioxide [except as provided in 27 CFR 24.319], nitrogen and oxygen)

- • Kind, quantity and date of use
- • Kind and volume of juice or wine in which used

Spirits Record
27 CFR 24.316

A proprietor who receives, stores, or uses spirits shall maintain a record of receipt and use. The record must show the following:

- • Date of receipt
- • From whom received
- • Kind of spirits
- • Proof gallons
- • Date and proof gallons of spirits used in wine production
- • Date and proof gallons of spirits removed from bonded wine premises and to whom

The proof gallons of spirits received, used, removed from bonded wine premises, and on hand at the end of the reporting period is reported on TTB Report of Wine Premises Operations Form 5120.17.

Production Issues

Chaptalization (Brix Adjustment), 27 CFR 24.177

The addition of sugar or concentrated juice of the same type of fruit to juice to adjust Brix before or during fermentation to develop alcohol by fermentation. Addition may not raise Brix above 25°. If ameliorating after chaptalization the quantity of dry sugar used is included as ameliorating material for grape wines; for fruit wines, the dry sugar does not count as ameliorating material, but the volume of water in liquid sugar or syrup does.

Amelioration, 27 CFR 4.21 and 27 CFR 24.178

The addition to juice or natural wine before, during or after fermentation, of either water or pure dry sugar or a combination, to adjust the acid level. Fixed acids may be not be reduced to below 5 grams/liter. For grapes and low acid fruit, the volume of the ameliorating material may not exceed 35% of the total volume; for high acid fruit or berries, the volume of the ameliorating material may not exceed 60% of the total. The maximum alcohol allowed for ameliorated wine is 13% for grape and agricultural wines and 14% for citrus and fruit wines. The maximum solids level is 22 grams/100 ml.

Sweetening, 27 CFR 24.179

The addition of juice, concentrated juice of the same type of fruit or sugar to wine after fermentation and before taxpayment. For grape wines that have not more than 14% alcohol, the finished wine may not exceed 17% solids; wines over 14% alcohol may not exceed 21% solids. For fruit wines, the finished wine may not exceed 21% solids or 14% alcohol. Specially sweetened wines may contain 17-35% solids but may not exceed 14% alcohol.

Concentrate/Juice, 27 CFR 24.180

Concentrate may be reduced before fermentation to anywhere between the original Brix and 22°. Juice that has been concentrated over 80° Brix may not be used. Unconcentrated fruit juice may be reduced to not less than 22° Brix.

Acids, 27 CFR 24.182

The acid level may be increased before, during or after fermentation. The type of acid used depends on the type of fruit and when it is added. The fixed acid level may not be increased over 9.0 grams/liter in the finished wine unless the solids are over 8 grams/100 ml, then the fixed acid can be increased to 11 grams/liter.

Materials, 27 CFR 24.246

Only the materials listed in 27 CFR 24.246 may be used in the production of wine, within the limitations listed, unless a formula is approved. Note that this list contains individual materials. Commercially prepared blends may only be used if all of the ingredients are on this list.

Processes, 27 CFR 24.248

Only the processes listed in 27 CFR 24.248 may be used in the production of wine. Note that many of the processes may only be done at a distilled spirits plant. The procedure for applying to experiment with a new material or process is given in 27 CFR 24.249, and the procedure for applying to add a new material or process is given in 27 CFR 24.250.

Bulk Still Wine Record
27 CFR 24.301

A proprietor who produces or receives still wine in bond must maintain a record of transactions for bulk still wine. A record is to be maintained for each tax class of still wine and must include date of transaction. The parts of 27 CFR 24.301 that usually pertain to Bonded Winery operations require the following information be recorded:

☐ The volume produced by fermentation in wine gallons, determined by actual measurement;

☐ The volume received, shipped taxpaid, removed (e.g., taxpaid, in bond, export, family use, samples) and used in sparkling wine production; if a tax credit under 26 U.S.C. 5041(c) may be claimed, the record will be maintained in sufficient detail to insure that such as tax credit is properly claimed;

☐ The specific type of production method used, e.g., natural fermentation, amelioration, sweetening, addition of spirits, blending;

☐ The volume of wine used and produced by amelioration, addition of spirits or sweetening, as determined by measurements of the wine before and after production;

☐ The volume of wine used for and produced by blending, if wines of different tax classes are blended together;

☐ The volume of wine used to produce formula wine, vinegar stock and distilling material;

☐ The volume of wine removed to fermenters for refermentation or removed directly to the production facilities of a distilled spirits plant or vinegar plant;

☐ Where a process authorized under 27 CFR 24.248 is employed, records will be maintained to allow for verification of any limitation specified for the process employed and to ensure that the use of the process is consistent with good commercial practice;

☐ Where a treating material is dissolved or dispersed in water as authorized in this part, the volume of water added to the wine; and

☐ An explanation of any unusual transactions.

Inventory Record
27 CFR 24.313

All bonded wineries and bonded wine cellars are required to take a complete physical inventory of all wine and spirits in storage on June 30. If a proprietor wishes to take the annual inventory on different date, TTB must be notified. Proprietors who file the Report Form 5120.17 annually must take the complete physical inventory at the end of the calendar year; quarterly filers must select an annual inventory period that begins on the first day of a calendar quarter. The inventory record must include the following information:

☐ Description of wine (name, vintage, varietal, appellation) and spirits; volume; tank number (bulk wine); summary of barrels and puncheons (bulk wine)

☐ Inventory Summary: volume of bulk wine and spirits and bottled wine totaled separately by tax class and reported on Form 5120.17

☐ Inventory Record: All pages will be numbered consecutively; the last page will be dated and signed, the last page will include the "Penalty of Perjury" statement: *"Under penalties of perjury, I declare that I have examined this inventory record and to the best of my knowledge and belief, it is a true, correct and complete record of all wine and spirits required to be inventoried."*

Inventory Losses
27 CFR 24.266

If the complete annual inventory of <u>bulk wine</u> reveals losses in production or storage which exceed the allowances listed below, a claim for allowance of loss must be filed on TTB Form 5620.8:

- Any losses due to theft, OR
- More than 3% of wine on hand at beginning of annual period and volume of wine received in bond, OR
- More than 6% of still wine produced by fermentation, OR
- More than 6% of sparkling wine produced in bottles, OR
- More than 3% of special natural wine (27 CFR 24.195), OR
- More than 3% of other wine (27 CFR 24.218), OR
- More than 3% of artificially carbonated wine, OR
- More than 3% of bulk processed sparkling wine

Normal bulk inventory losses due to racking, evaporation and topping are to be reported on the Report of Wine Premises Operations in Section A, Line 30.

<u>Bottled wine losses must be taxpaid:</u> If the proprietor has conducted a complete physical inventory, the tax on any unexplained losses of untaxpaid bottled or packed wine must be paid.

Note: Documented casualty losses are NOT "inventory losses." They are reported to TTB as they occur.

Other Records Required by 27 CFR Part 24, Subpart O

The operations of bonded wineries may require maintaining some of the records listed below. Please refer to the text of the regulations to determine if the record should be maintained.

Effervescent Wine Record, 27 CFR 24.302

Formula Wine Record, 27 CFR 24.303

Chaptalization (Brix Adjustment) and Amelioration Record, 27 CFR 24.304

Sweetening Record, 27 CFR 24.305

Distilling Materials or Vinegar Stock Record, 27 CFR 24.306

Nonbeverage Wine Record, 27 CFR 24.307

Unmerchantable Wine Record, 27 CFR 24.312

Carbon Dioxide Record, 27 CFR 24.319

Decolorizing Material Record, 27 CFR 24.321

Allied Products Record, 27 CFR 24.322

142

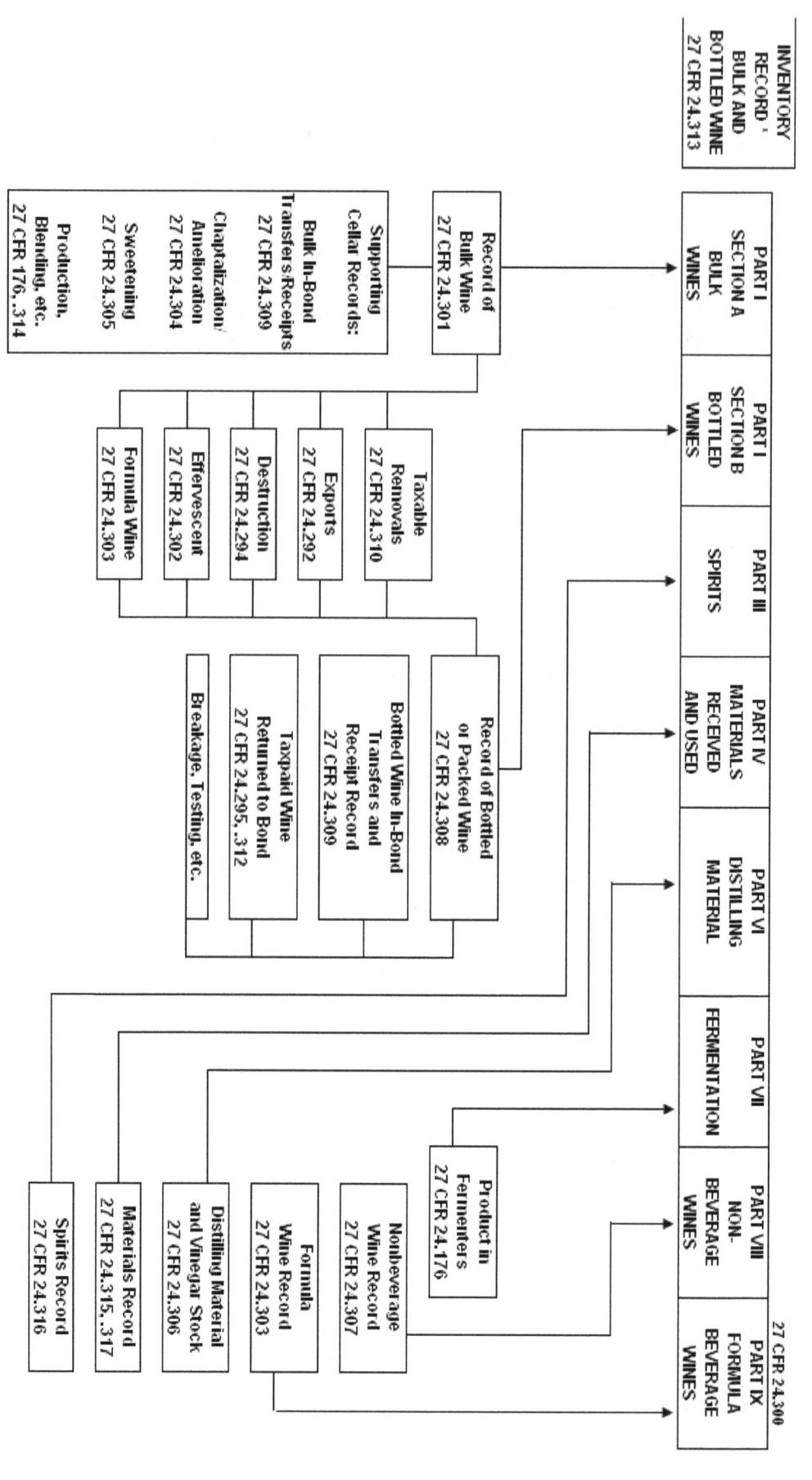

FORM 5120.17 - REPORT OF WINE PREMISES OPERATIONS

INVENTORY RECORD¹ BULK AND BOTTLED WINE 27 CFR 24.313

PART I SECTION A BULK WINES

PART I SECTION B BOTTLED WINES

PART III SPIRITS

PART IV MATERIALS RECEIVED AND USED

PART VI DISTILLING MATERIAL

PART VII FERMENTATION

PART VIII NON-BEVERAGE WINES

27 CFR 24.300 PART IX FORMULA BEVERAGE WINES

Record of Bulk Wine 27 CFR 24.301

Supporting Cellar Records:

Bulk In-Bond Transfers:Receipts 27 CFR 24.309

Chaptalization/ Amelioration 27 CFR 24.304

Sweetening 27 CFR 24.305

Production, Blending, etc. 27 CFR 176, .314

Taxable Removals 27 CFR 24.310

Exports 27 CFR 24.292

Destruction 27 CFR 24.294

Effervescent 27 CFR 24.302

Formula Wine 27 CFR 24.303

Record of Bottled or Packed Wine 27 CFR 24.308

Bottled Wine In-Bond Transfers and Receipt Record 27 CFR 24.309

Taxpaid Wine Returned to Bond 27 CFR 24.295, .312

Breakage, Testing, etc.

Product in Fermenters 27 CFR 24.176

Nonbeverage Wine Record 27 CFR 24.307

Distilling Material and Vinegar Stock 27 CFR 24.306

Formula Wine Record 27 CFR 24.303

Spirits Record 27 CFR 24.316

Materials Record 27 CFR 24.315, .317

¹ An inventory is required on June 30 for proprietors filing Monthly or Quarterly Reports and December 31 if filing Annual Reports.

Here are two examples of batch records that would meet TTB recordkeeping requirements:

2008 Napa Valley Sauvignon Blanc

Date	Activity	Tank	Volume	Comments
9/10/2008	Crush/press 30 ppm SO2 added	116	~4000	100% Estate Vineyard 100% SB, Napa Valley 100% 2008, 23.4 tons 23.1 Brix, TA 0.8, pH 3.07
9/11/2008	Crush/press 30 ppm SO2 added	117	~4000	100% Estate Vineyard 100% SB, Napa Valley 100% 2008, 23.5 tons 23.2 Brix, TA 0.8, pH 3.10
9/12/2008	Rack T-116 & 117 off lees, inoculate	125	~8000	100% Estate Vineyard 100 SB, Napa Valley 100% 2008
9/20/2008	Add 12# bentonite	125	~8000	
10/3/2008	Rack T-125 off fermentation lees Declare Produced 20 ppm SO2 added	130	7504	100% Estate Vineyard 100% SB, Napa Valley 100% 2008 14.04% alc, TA 0.65, pH 3.30, SO2 25/50; 470 gal lees
10/7/2008	Add 62.25# Tartaric Acid	130	7504	TA 0.74, pH 3.22
11/15/2008	Rack & blend with 1400 gal. 2006 CA Dry White from Pleasant Day Vyds. 10 ppm SO2 added	100	8875	29 gallon loss 94.9% SB, Napa Valley 100% 2008, 13.8% alc. TA 0.70, pH 3.28, SO2 28/58
11/17/2008	Add 26.5# bentonite	100	8903	28 gallon gain
12/10/2008	DE filter off lees	101	8873	30 gallons lees
12/31/2008	Inventory	101	8873	
1/15/2009	DE filter off tartrates	105	8865	8 gallon loss 13.8% alc, TA 0.60, pH 3.40, SO2 28/58
1/21/2009	Add 110.25# Malic acid	105	8870	5 gallon gain 13.8% alc, TA 0.77, pH 3.25
2/2/2009	Bottle: 3729 cs 750 mL 8865.8 gallons			4 gallon loss COLA 07-01 13.8% alc, TA 0.77, pH 3.25 Fill: 751, 750, 751, 749 mL

~Sample Record~

LOT 08-SB-01
2008 Sauvignon Blanc

~Sample Record~

Date	Vineyard/Grower	W Tag	Variety/Tons	Tank	Volume	Brix	TA	pH	VA(g/L)	Alc	Vintage, Varietal, Appellation
9/10/08	NV/Estate	M 1246	SB 12.09	116	2,050	23.1°	0.8	3.07	---	---	100% Estate vyd., 100% Napa Valley SB, 100% 2008
9/11/08	NV/Estate	M 1247	SB 11.31	116	1,920	23.1°	0.8	3.07	---	---	100% Estate vyd., 100% Napa Valley SB, 100% 2008
9/11/08	NV/Estate	M 1248	SB 12.51	117	2,120	23.1°	0.8	3.10	---	---	SB, 100% 2008
9/11/08	NV/Estate	M 1249	SB 10.99	117	1,970	23.3°	0.8	3.10	---	---	

Date	Operation	Tank	Vol Beg	Vol End	Gain/Loss	TA	pH	VA(g/L)	Alc	Comments	Vintage, Varietal, Appellation
9/10/08	Crush/press 23.4 tons SB; 30 ppm SO2 added	116	0	~4000		0.8	3.07			East side of vyd	
9/11/08	Crush/press 23.5 tons SB; 30 ppm SO2 added	117	0	~4000		0.8	3.10			West side of vyd	
9/12/08	Rack 116 & 117 to 125, inoculate	125	0	~8000						Rack off lees	
9/20/08	Add 12# bentonite	125	~8000	~8000				0.1			
10/3/08	Rack 125 to 130, 20 ppm SO2 added	130	0	7504		0.65	3.30			Declare produced, 470 gal. lees	
10/7/08	Add 62.25# tartaric acid	130	7504	7504		0.74	3.22				
11/15/08	Rack	100	7504	7504			3.28				
11/15/08	Blend with 1400 gal 2008 Dry White, add 10 ppm SO2	100	7504	8875	-29	0.7					94.9% SB, 94.9% Napa Valley, 100% 2008
11/17/08	Add 26.5# bentonite	100	8875	8903	28						
12/10/08	DE filter off lees	101	8873							30 gal lees	
12/31/08	Inventory	101	8873								
1/15/09	DE filter off tartrates	105	8865	8865	-8	0.6	3.40				
1/21/09	Add 110.25# Malic Acid	105	8865	8870	5	0.77	3.25				
2/2/09	Bottle	Bot. Rm.	8870	0	-4.2	0.77	3.25	0.1		COLA 06-01	
	750 mL 3729 cs.									Fill: 751, 750, 751, 749 mL	

Form 5120.17, Report of Wine Premises Operations
27 CFR 24.300 (g)

The Heading:

- Enter the month the report covers, or the quarter or year, if filing a quarterly or annual report.
- Enter the Registry Number of your premises in this format: "BW-XX-XXXX."
- Write in your Employer Identification Number (EIN) at the top of the page, near the Registry Number, in this format: "94-xxxxxxx."
- Enter the name of the wine premises as shown on your registration documents, the address of the premises, and the telephone number.

Section A – Bulk Wines:

- On Line 1 in each column, enter the "On Hand End of Period" figure from Line 31 of the previous report.
- Lines 2 through 11 are activities which add to your bulk inventory.
- Lines 13 through 30 are activities which decrease the bulk inventory.
- Line 31 is a book inventory figure of the amount of bulk wine on hand at the end of the period. It is the actual amount only after physical inventory adjustments are made.
- For purposes of this report, "Blending" means the mixing together of wines from two or more tax classes. The total of the figures entered in Lines 5 and 20 should equal.
- A change in tax class resulting from testing alcohol content rather than by blending is shown as an increase in the amount of wine in the column representing the correct tax class, written into Line 10 or 11. The same amount is shown as a decrease from the amount of wine in the incorrect column, written into one of the Lines 24-28.
- The amount shown as "Bottled" in Line 13 must equal the amount shown in Section B – Bottled Wines – Line 2.

Section B – Bottled Wines:

- On Line 1 of each column, enter the "On Hand End of Period" figure from Line 20 of the previous report.
- Lines 2 through 6 are activities which add to your bottled inventory.
- Lines 8 through 19 are activities which decrease the bottled inventory.
- Line 20 is a book inventory figure of the amount of bottled wine on hand at the end of the period. It is the actual amount only after physical inventory adjustments are made.
- The amount of wine shown as Removed Taxpaid on Line 8 must agree with the excise taxes paid on Form(s) 5000.24 for the period.
- Bottled inventory shortages shown on Line 19 must be tax paid or satisfactorily explained.

Back of the Report Form:

- Part III – Show the receipt and use of Distilled Spirits, if any, in proof gallons and not in standard gallons. Remember that the tax liability of distilled spirits is $13.50 per proof gallons and may affect your bond coverage.
- Part IV – Show the receipt and use of Wine Making Materials in pounds or gallons. The volume used in wine production should be moved to Part VII if it is still fermenting at the end of the reporting period, or measured and moved to the front of the report as "produced." See 27 CFR 24.176(b) about determining wine produced.
- Part VI – Show the production, receipt and use of Distilling Material and Vinegar Stock, if any.
- Part VII – When wine making materials are still in fermentation at the end of the reporting period, estimate the volume for each type of fruit and enter the amount in this section.
- Parts VIII and IX – Enter the amount of non-beverage, vermouth, special natural or formula wines produced and withdrawn, if any.
- Part X – Use this space to explain any unusual transactions.

On the following pages, you will find a line-by-line guide to the Report of Wine Premises Operations Form 5120.17. It may be found on our website at this link:

http://www.ttb.gov/wine/new_guide.shtml

Section and Line of Form 5120.17	Useful Regulations	How the Spaces are Completed

FRONT OF FORM 5120.17

PART 1 - SUMMARY OF WINES IN BOND (GALLONS)		
SECTION A - BULK WINES	27 CFR 24.301	Lines 2-11 represent increases in the amount of wine to be accounted for in the bulk wine account. Lines 13-30 represent decreases in this amount.
1 ON HAND BEGINNING OF PERIOD		Enter the same amounts that were shown on Line 31 in each column of the last report submitted.
2 PRODUCED BY FERMENTATION	24.301(a); 24.302	Columns (a), (b), (d) and (f): When fermentation is complete or the material used for wine is removed from the fermenter, the volume is entered here. The volume must be accurately measured and the alcohol content determined. If the wine contains lees, the entire volume of the storage container (ie: barrel) must be entered; the lees will be removed at a later date and included among inventory losses. Column (e): This is sparkling wine in tirage. Enter the amount of Bottle Fermented Sparkling Wine produced in the space marked "BF" and the amount of Bulk Processed Sparkling Wine produced in the space marked "BP."
3 PRODUCED BY SWEETENING	24.301(d); 24.305	This is the amount of wine which has had sweetening materials added to it. The amount of wine listed in Sec A Line 18 is the amount BEFORE the addition of sweetening materials; this is the amount AFTER the addition.
4 PRODUCED BY ADDITION OF WINE SPIRITS	24.301(d)	This is the amount of wine which has had wine spirits added to it. The amount listed in Sec A Line 19 is the amount BEFORE the addition of spirits; this is the amount AFTER the addition. Be sure to verify the alcohol content of the wine after the addition of spirits, and place the result in the proper column.
5 PRODUCED BY BLENDING	24.301(e)	"Blending" for TTB recordkeeping purposes means wine from two or more tax classes was mixed together. The amount of wine listed Sec A Line 20 is the amount BEFORE blending; this is the amount AFTER blending. (Example: In Sec A Line 20, enter 100 gallons of -14% wine and 300 gallons of 14%-21% wine used for blending. If the alcohol content of the blend is 14%-21%, enter 400 gallons in Sec A Line 7 Col (b)).
6 PRODUCED BY AMELIORATION	24.301(d); 24.304	This is the amount of wine which has had ameliorating materials added to it. The amount of wine listed in Sec A Line 21 is the amount BEFORE the addition of ameliorating materials; this is the amount AFTER the addition.
7 RECEIVED IN BOND	24.301(b)	Record the amount of untaxpaid bulk wine received from another bonded winery or bonded wine cellar here.
8 BOTTLED WINE DUMPED TO BULK	24.308(a)	This is the amount of bottled wine that was emptied into the bulk wine account. The same amount is reported in Sec B, Line 10, below.
9 INVENTORY GAIN	24.313	If you discover that your actual bulk inventory is greater than the "book" figure carried in your records, make the increasing adjustment here. This is to be done only when a complete physical inventory of all wine is conducted.
10 *Write-in Entry:* Change of Tax Class	24.301	This entry is used to move an amount of wine from one column (tax class) to another when it is discovered that the alcohol content is not what was previously reported, and when sparkling wine is returned to the still wine account. Show the same amount before the change in one of the blank lines below (Sec A Lines 24-28).
11 *Write-in Entry:* Formula Wine Produced	24.301(f); 24.303	Use this line to show the amount of Formula Wine Produced, AFTER the addition of flavors and other materials to the base wine. The wine used for the production of Formula Wine is shown as a write-in entry on a blank line, Sec A Lines 24-28, below.
Other Write-in: Slurry Gain	24.301(i)	Use this space to account for gains due to the use of a slurry solution produced with water.
Other Write-in: Recovered from Lees		Use this space to add wine recovered from the pressing of lees.
12 TOTAL		This is the sum of Line 1 + the amounts given in Lines 2-11.

148

13	BOTTLED	24.308	Enter the amount of wine bottled and packed during the period. The same amount is shown in Sec B, Line 2, below. <u>Column (e)</u>: Enter the amount of finished (disgorged) Bottle Fermented Sparkling Wine bottled in the space marked "BF," and the amount of finished (disgorged) Bulk Process Sparkling Wine bottled in the space marked "BP."
14	REMOVED TAXPAID	24.301(b); 24.310	Enter the amount of bulk wine taxably removed during the period.
15	TRANSFERS IN BOND	24.301(b); 24.309	Record the amount of untaxpaid bulk wine shipped to another bonded winery or bonded wine cellar here.
16	REMOVED FOR DISTILLING MATERIAL	24.301(g); 24.306	Enter the amount removed to a distilled spirits plant or another bonded wine premises that will be used as distilling material. Show the same figure on the back of the form in Part VI, Lines 2 and 6 or 7.
17	REMOVED TO VINEGAR PLANT	24.301(g); 24.306	Enter the amount removed to a vinegar plant. Show the same figure on the back of the form in Part VI, Lines 2 and 7 or 8.
18	USED FOR SWEETENING	24.301(d); 24.305	This is the amount of wine that had sweetening materials added to it. The amount of wine listed in Sec A Line 3 is the amount AFTER the addition of sweetening materials; this is the amount BEFORE the addition.
19	USED FOR ADDITION OF WINE SPIRITS	24.301(d)	This is the amount of wine that had wine spirits added to it. The amount of wine listed in Sec A Line 4 above is the amount AFTER the addition of the spirits; this is the amount BEFORE the addition.
20	USED FOR BLENDING	24.301(e)	"Blending" for TTB recordkeeping purposes means wine from two or more tax classes was mixed together. The amount of wine listed in sec A Line 5 is the amount AFTER blending; this is the amount BEFORE blending. (Example: if 100 gallons of -14% wine is blended with 300 gallons of 14%-21%, show the amounts in Col (a) and (b) on this line. If the alcohol content of the blend is 14%-21%, enter the 400 gallons in Sec A Line 7 Col (b)), above.)
21	USED FOR AMELIORATION	24.301(d); 24.304	This is the amount of wine that had ameliorating materials added to it. The amount of wine listed in Sec A Line 6 is the amount AFTER the addition of ameliorating materials; this is the amount BEFORE the addition.
22	USED FOR EFFERVESCENT WINE	24.301(b); 24.302	This is the amount of still wine used for effervescent (sparkling or artificially carbonated) wine. Show the amount of effervescent wine produced in Sec A Line 2 Col. (d) or (e)(BF or BP), as appropriate.
23	USED FOR TESTING	24.95-.97	Enter the amount of wine used for testing. Testing may take place on or off the bonded premises.
24	*Write-In Entry:* Change of Tax Class	24.301	This entry is used to move an amount of wine from one column (tax class) to another when it is discovered that the alcohol content is not what was previously reported, and when sparkling wine is returned to the still wine account. Show the same amount after the change as a write-in entry in Sec A Line 10 or 11, above. Do this whenever you learn that the tax class of a wine has been reported incorrectly.
25	*Write-In Entry:* Used for Formula Wine Production	24.301(f); 24.303	Use this line to show the amount of base wine used for the production of a Formula Wine, BEFORE the addition of flavors and other materials to the base wine. The finished amount of Formula Wine produced AFTER the addition of flavors and other materials is shown as a write-in entry in Sec A Line 10 or 11, above.
26	*Write-In Entry:* Removed for Export	24.301(b); 27 CFR 28	When untaxpaid bulk wine is exported out of the U.S., enter the amount as a write-in entry. Submit TTB Export Form 5100.11 and proof of export for each shipment.
27	*Write-In Entry:* Returned to Fermenter	24.301(g)	Show the amount of bulk wine returned to a fermenter for refermentation here.
28	*Write-In Entry:* Used for Non-beverage wine	24.307	This is the amount of wine that had materials added which render the wine unfit for beverage use. The amount of wine listed in Part VIII is the amount AFTER the addition of materials; this is the amount BEFORE the addition.
	Other Write-in: Removed to DM or VS Account	24.301(f) ; 24.306	Show the removal from the bulk wine account the amount of wine designated for use as distilling material or vinegar stock. Show corresponding entries on Part VI, Line 2 on reverse of report form.
	Other Write-in: Destroyed	24.294	Before destroying any wine, obtain permission from TTB. After receiving approval from TTB and destroying the wine, show the amount destroyed.
29	LOSSES (OTHER THAN INVENTORY)	24.268	Report casualty losses on this line, such as spillage due to equipment failure. Casualty losses must be reported to TTB, and a claim may need to be submitted.
30	INVENTORY LOSSES	24.266; 24.313	Use this line to balance the report with the actual amount of wine on hand. This is to be done only when a complete physical inventory of all wine is conducted. If you discover that your actual bulk inventory is less than the "book" figure carried in your records, make the decreasing adjustment here. Include the normal operational topping, racking, evaporation, lees removal and bottling losses that occur throughout the year. [Note: a complete physical inventory must be taken once each year.] A claim must be filed with TTB if annual inventory losses exceed the allowable limits given in 27 CFR 24.266.
31	ON HAND END OF PERIOD		This is the amount of bulk wine in storage at the end of the period in each tax class. It is a "book" figure for most of the year. The "actual" amount on hand is entered when a complete inventory of all untaxpaid wine is taken and you make adjusting entries above. Carry this figure forward to Sec A Line 1 of the next report filed. This is the sum of Line 12 minus the amounts given in Lines 13-30.
32	TOTAL		This figure is the total of lines 13 through 31. It agrees with the figure on line 12.

	SECTION B - BOTTLED WINE	27 CFR 24.308	Lines 2-6 represent increases in the amount of wine to be accounted for in the bottled wine account. Lines 8-19 represent decreases in this amount.
1	ON HAND BEGINNING OF PERIOD		Enter the same amounts that were shown on Line 20 of this section in each column of the last report submitted.
2	BOTTLED	24.308	Enter the amount of wine bottled and packed during the period. The same amount is shown in Sec A, Line13, above. Column (e): Enter the amount of finished (disgorged) Bottle Fermented Sparkling Wine bottled in the space marked "BF," and the amount of finished (disgorged) Bulk Process Sparkling Wine bottled in the space marked "BP."
3	RECEIVED IN BOND	24.309	Record the amount of untaxpaid bottled wine received from another bonded winery or bonded wine cellar here.
4	TAXPAID WINE RETURNED TO BOND	24.312	Enter the amount of of taxpaid wine returned to the bonded premises. File a claim in accordance with 27 CFR 24.66 to request a refund or credit of the tax.
5	Inventory Gain (Write-in Entry)	24.313	When the annual physical inventory reveals a gain of bottled wine, make the adjustment on this line as a write-in entry. Do not report bottled inventory gains unless a complete inventory of all bulk and bottled wine is taken. [Note: a complete physical inventory must be taken once each year.]
6	(blank line)		
7	TOTAL		This is the sum of Line 1+ the amounts given in Lines 2-6.
8	REMOVED TAXPAID	24.270; 24.310	Enter the amount of bottled wine taxably removed during the period.
9	TRANSFERRED IN BOND	24.280; 24.309	Record the amount of untaxpaid bottled wine shipped to another bonded winery or bonded wine cellar here.
10	DUMPED TO BULK	24.308(a)	This is the amount of bottled wine that was emptied and entered into the bulk wine account. The same amount is reported in Sec A, Line 8, above.
11	USED FOR TASTING	24.97	This is the amount of wine poured for tasting when winery's tasting room is on the bonded premises. If the tasting room is not part of the bonded premises, the amount used for tasting must be shown as a taxable removal on Line 8 of this Section.
12	REMOVED FOR EXPORT	27 CFR 28	When untaxpaid bottled wine is exported out of the U.S., enter the amount on this line. Submit TTB Export Form 5100.11 and proof of export for each shipment.
13	REMOVED FOR FAMILY USE	24.75	Wine may be removed untaxpaid for family use by individual owners and partnerships (not corporations). The amount is limited to 100 gallons per year if there is one adult in the household, or a maximum of 200 gallons if there are two or more adults in the household.
14	USED FOR TESTING	24.95	Enter the amount of wine used for testing. Testing may take place on or off the bonded premises.
15	Write-in Entry: Destroyed	24.294	After receiving approval from TTB, show the amount of bottled wine destroyed.
16	(blank line)		
17	(blank line)		
18	BREAKAGE	24.308(a)	If bottled wine is destroyed by breakage, report the amount here.
19	INVENTORY SHORTAGE	24.266; 24.313	When the annual physical inventory reveals a shortage of bottled wine, report the amount here. Wine excise tax must be paid on bottled inventory shortages. Do not report bottled inventory shortages unless a complete inventory of all bulk and bottled wine is taken. [Note: a complete physical inventory must be taken once each year.]
20	ON HAND END OF PERIOD		This is the amount of bottled wine in storage at the end of the period in each tax class. It is a "book" figure for most of the year, and the "actual" amount on hand when a complete inventory of all untaxpaid wine is taken and you make adjusting entries above. Carry this figure forward to Sec B Line 1 of the next report filed. This is the sum of Line 7 minus the amounts given in Lines 8-19.
21	TOTAL		This figure is the total of lines 8 through 20. It agrees with the figure on line 7.

150

BACK OF THE FORM

PART II - (RESERVED)

PART III - SUMMARY OF DISTILLED SPIRITS (PROOF GALLONS) - 27 CFR 24.316

		Col. (a)-(d): Wine Spirits for Addition to Wine
		Col. (e): Wine Spirits for Preparation of Dosages or Essences
		Col. (f)-(g): Distillates Containing Aldehydes
		Col. (h): Spirits For Use in Non-Beverage Wines
1	ON HAND BEGINNING OF PERIOD	Enter the same amount of proof gallons that were shown on Line 9 of this section in each column of the last report submitted.
2	RECEIVED	Enter the amount of proof gallons of distilled spirits received during the period in each column, as appropriate.
3	INVENTORY GAIN	If you discover that your distilled spirits inventory is greater than the "book" figure carried in your records, make the increasing adjustment here. A physical inventory of spirits storage tanks must be taken at the close of any month during which spirits were used in wine production, or when use of spirits for the month is completed, per 24.236.
4	TOTAL	This is the sum of Line 1 + the amounts given in Lines 2-3.
5	USED	Enter the amount of proof gallons of spirits used in each column, as appropriate.
6	TRANS. TO COL. (e)	Col. (a)-(d): Enter the amount of proof gallons of spirits used for preparation of dosages or essences.
7	*(blank line)*	Use this line to report other removals of distilled spirits, if necessary.
8	LOSSES	Report any losses revealed by physical inventory here. File a claim as shown in 27 CFR 24.65 for remission of the tax on the spirits.
9	ON HAND END OF PERIOD	This is the amount of proof gallons of distilled spirits in storage at the end of the period in each category. Carry this figure forward to Line 1 of this part on the next report filed. This is the sum of Line 4 minus the amounts given in Lines 5-8.
10	TOTAL	This is the same figure shown in Line 4.

PART IV - SUMMARY OF MATERIALS RECEIVED AND USED - 27 CFR 24.315

		Col. (a): Pounds of Uncrushed Grapes
		Col. (b): Gallons of Field Crushed Grapes
		Col. (c): Gallons of Grape Juice
		Col. (d): Gallons of Grape Concentrate
		Col. (e)-(g): Pounds or Gallons of Materials other than Grape
		Col. (h): Pounds of Dry Sugar
		Col. (i) Gallons of Liquid Sugar
1	ON HAND BEGINNING OF PERIOD	Enter the same amounts that were shown on Line 9 of this section in each column of the last report submitted.
2	RECEIVED	Enter the amount of materials received during the period in each column, as appropriate.
3	JUICE OR CONCENTRATE PRODUCED	Enter the amount of juice/concentrate produced during the period.
4	TOTAL	This is the sum of Line 1 + the amounts given in Lines 2-3
5	USED IN WINE PRODUCTION	Show the pounds/gallons used in the production of wine during the period here. Enter the amount of wine making material that is still fermenting at the end of the period in Part VII, or the amount produced in Part I Section A Line 2.
6	USED IN JUICE OR CONCENTRATE PRODUCTION	Show the pounds/gallons used in the production of juice or concentrate here. Enter the amount of juice/concentrate produced in this Section, Line 3.
7	USED IN ALLIED PRODUCTS	Enter the pounds/gallons used in the production of allied products (commercial fruit products and by-products, including volatile fruit-flavor concentrate) here.
8	REMOVED	Enter the pounds/gallons removed from the bonded premises.
9	ON HAND END OF PERIOD	This is the amount of winemaking materials in storage at the end of the period in each category. Carry this figure forward to Line 1 of this part on the next report filed. This is the sum of Line 4 minus the amounts given in Lines 5-8.
10	TOTAL	This is the same figure shown in Line 4.

PART V - (RESERVED)

		PART VI - SUMMARY OF DISTILLING MATERIAL AND VINEGAR STOCK (Gallons) - 27 CFR 24.216-.217
		Col. (a)-(b): Distilling Material
		Col. (c)-(d): Vinegar Stock
1	ON HAND BEGINNING OF PERIOD (Storage Tanks)	Enter the same amounts that were shown on Line 10 of this section in each column of the last report submitted.
2	PRODUCED	Enter the same amounts that were shown in Part 1, Section A, Lines 16-17, and as a write-in entry in Sec A Lines 24-28 (Removed to the DM/VS account).
3	RECEIVED FROM OTHER BONDED WINE PREMISES	Enter the amount received, as appropriate.
4	(blank line)	This line may be used to show an inventory gain or other receipt.
5	TOTAL	This is the sum of Line 1 + the amounts given in Lines 2-4
6	REMOVED TO DISTILLED SPIRITS PLANTS	Enter the amount of distilling material removed to a distilled spirits plant, shown in Sec A Line 16.
7	REMOVED TO OTHER BONDED WINE PREMISES	Enter the amount removed to other bonded wine premises, shown in Sec A Lines 16-17.
8	REMOVED TO VINEGAR PLANTS	Enter the amount of vinegar stock removed to vinegar plants, shown in Sec A Line 17
9	(blank line)	This may be used to show inventory shortage, loss or other removals.
10	ON HAND END OF PERIOD (Storage Tanks)	This is the amount of distilling material and vinegar stock in storage at the end of the period. Carry this figure forward to Line 1 of this part on the next report filed. This is the sum of Line 5 minus the amounts given in Lines 6-9.
11	TOTAL	This is the same figure shown in Line 5.

		PART VII - IN FERMENTERS END OF PERIOD (Gallons)
1	IN FERMENTERS (ESTIMATED QUANTITY OF LIQUID)	When the fermentation of materials used for wine production is not complete at the end of the reporting period, enter an estimate of the amount in fermenters here. Use Columns (a)-(e) to indicate different types of winemaking materials, such as grapes, apples, blackberries, etc. When fermentation is complete, enter the specific amount produced in Part I Section A Line 2.

		PART VIII - SUMMARY OF NONBEVERAGE WINES (Gallons) - 27 CFR 24.215
		Col. (a): Nonbeverage wines containing not over 14% alcohol
		Col. (b): Nonbeverage wines containing 14-21% alcohol
		Col. (c): Total of Columns (a) and (b).
1	PRODUCED	This is the amount of wine which has had materials added to it which render the wine unfit for beverage use. The amount of wine listed as a write-in entry in Section A is the amount BEFORE the addition of materials; this is the amount AFTER the addition.
2	WITHDRAWN	Enter the amount of nonbeverage wine removed from the bonded premises.

		PART IX - SPECIAL NATURAL WINES AND 27 CFR 24.218 WINES (Gallons) - 27 CFR 24.195 and 24.218
		Col. (a): Vermouth
		Col. (b)-(e): Other Special Natural Wines
		Col. (f): Total of Columns (a)-(e)
		Col. (g): Other than Standard Wines
1	PRODUCED	Enter the amount of Vermouth, other Special Natural Wines and Other than Standard Wines produced during the period.
2	TAXABLE REMOVALS	Enter the amount of Vermouth, other Special Natural Wines and Other than Standard Wines taxably removed during the period.
3	ON HAND END OF PERIOD	This is the amount of Vermouth, other Special Natural Wines and Other than Standard Wines on the bonded premises at the end of the period.

		PART X - REMARKS
		Use this space to report any unusual transactions or to state that another report will not be filed until reportable operations take place.

		NAME OF PROPRIETOR, SIGNATURE/TITLE, DATE
	Proprietor	Give the name of company.
	By (Signature and Title)	Signer of the report must have Signature Authority on file with TTB.
	Date	Give the date the report was completed.

Report Filing Dates

The Report of Wine Premises Operations Form 5120.17 is due 15 days after the close of the period, i.e. by the 15th of the next month if filing monthly; by January 15th if filing annually; or by April 15th, July 15th, October 15th or January 15th if filing quarterly.

If you file reports on the monthly basis but do not expect to have any reportable operations in the next month(s), you may indicate that on the report being filed and wait until operations commence before filing the next report.

Eligibility for an Annual Report:

If you file an annual tax return **and** if the total of your bulk and bottled wine does not exceed 20,000 gallons at any time, you may file an annual report.

The annual report is due January 15th following the close of the year.

If you exceed the $1,000/year limit in excise tax (eligibility for filing an annual tax return) **or** the 20,000 gallons on-hand limit, you must file the reports on the monthly basis for the rest of the year. You may be eligible for filing Quarterly Reports and/or returns.

Eligibility for a Quarterly Report:

If you file quarterly tax returns **and** if the total of your bulk and bottled wine does not exceed 60,000 gallons at any time, you may file quarterly reports.

The quarterly reports are due April 15th, July 15th, October 15th and January 15th .

If you exceed the $50,000/year limit in excise tax (the eligibility for filing a quarterly tax return) **or** the 60,000 gallons on-hand limit, you must file the reports on the monthly basis for the rest of the year.

OMB No. 1513-0053 (8/31/2005)

DEPARTMENT OF THE TREASURY
ALCOHOL AND TOBACCO TAX AND TRADE BUREAU (TTB)
REPORT OF WINE PREMISES OPERATIONS

PERIOD
MONTH _____ (Month) YEAR _____ 2006
(If applicable)

REGISTRY NUMBER _____
BW-(State)-xxxx

OPERATED BY (Name, Address and Telephone)
Operating Name of Wine Premises
Address
Telephone Number
EIN: 99-999999x

INSTRUCTIONS

1. The reporting period for this form shall be monthly, except that proprietors who qualify under the exception stated in 27 CFR 24.300 (g)(2) may file this form on a calendar year basis unless required to file monthly by the Alcohol and Tobacco Tax and Trade Bureau (TTB). A proprietor who files monthly reports but does not expect any reportable operations in a subsequent month or months may indicate in Part X that no monthly reports will be filed until a reportable operation occurs. (§24.300 (g)(1))

2. Prepare this form in duplicate and file it by the fifteenth day after the end of the report period (month or year). Keep the copy on your bonded wine premises for inspection by TTB officers. Send the original to TTB at this address.

Director, National Revenue Center
Alcohol and Tobacco Tax and Trade Bureau
550 Main St. Ste 8002
Cincinnati, OH 45202-5215

3. Explain any unusual operations in Part X.

4. The quantities "on hand end" will ordinarily be "book inventory" figures, that is the quantity required to balance each summary. Use the "on hand end" from your report for the previous period as the "on hand beginning" of the current report. On reports for any period when you take a physical inventory, report the difference as losses for bulk wine and shortages for bottled wine, or as gains, as the case may be.

5. If the quantity of wine previously reported on TTB F 5120.17 is affected by adjustments made on a tax return, TTB F 5000.24, adjust the current TTB F 5120.17 in Section A, (and Section B, if bottled wine is involved). Explain the entries in Part X.

PART I - SUMMARY OF WINES IN BOND (GALLONS)

ITEM	ALCOHOL CONTENT BY VOLUME			ARTIFICIALLY CARBONATED WINE (d)	SPARKLING WINE (e)	HARD CIDER (f)
	NOT OVER 14 PERCENT (a)	OVER 14 TO 21 PERCENT (Inclusive) (b)	OVER 21 TO 24 PERCENT (Inclusive) (c)			
SECTION A - BULK WINES						
1 ON HAND BEGINNING OF PERIOD	105,000	150				0
2 PRODUCED BY FERMENTATION	22,600				BF / BP	1,200
3 PRODUCED BY SWEETENING						
4 PRODUCED BY ADDITION OF WINE SPIRITS		325				
5 PRODUCED BY BLENDING		230				
6 PRODUCED BY AMELIORATION						
7 RECEIVED IN BOND	600					
8 BOTTLED WINE DUMPED TO BULK	285					
9 INVENTORY GAINS						
10						
11						
12 TOTAL	128,485	705				1,200
13 BOTTLED	2,378				BF / BP	
14 REMOVED TAXPAID						
15 TRANSFERS IN BOND						
16 REMOVED FOR DISTILLING MATERIAL						
17 REMOVED TO VINEGAR PLANT						
18 USED FOR SWEETENING						
19 USED FOR ADDITION OF WINE SPIRITS	300					
20 USED FOR BLENDING	115	115				
21 USED FOR AMELIORATION						
22 USED FOR EFFERVESCENT WINE						
23 USED FOR TESTING						
24						
25						
26						
27						
28						
29 LOSSES (OTHER THAN INVENTORY)						
30 INVENTORY LOSSES						
31 ON HAND END OF PERIOD	125,692	590				1,200
32 TOTAL	128,485	705				1,200
SECTION B - BOTTLED WINES						
1 ON HAND BEGINNING OF PERIOD	50,070	59				
2 BOTTLED	2,378				BF / BP	
3 RECEIVED IN BOND						
4 TAXPAID WINE RETURNED TO BOND	59					
5						
6						
7 TOTAL	52,507	59				
8 REMOVED TAXPAID	1,189	5				
9 TRANSFERRED IN BOND						
10 DUMPED TO BULK	285					
11 USED FOR TASTING	7					
12 REMOVED FOR EXPORT	119					
13 REMOVED FOR FAMILY USE						
14 USED FOR TESTING						
15						
16						
17						
18 BREAKAGE						
19 INVENTORY SHORTAGE						
20 ON HAND END OF PERIOD	50,907	54				
21 TOTAL	52,807	59				

TTB F 5120.17 (5/2005)

1 These lines, (e) on line marked "BF" the quantity of sparkling wine produced by fermentation in bottles, and on line mark "BP" the quantity of sparkling wine produced by bulk process.

2 Section A line 1 and Section B line 2 should show the same quantities. Enter in col (e) on line marked "BF" the quantity of finished bottle-fermented sparkling wine bottled, and on line marked "BP" the quantity of finished bulk-process wine bottled.

3 Fully explain in either Part X, or on a separate signed statement submitted with this report. Failure to immediately explain shortages of bottled wine may result in the assessment of taxes applicable to those shortages.

4 Only report blending of wines of different tax classes as is blended together.

PART II - (RESERVED)

PART III - SUMMARY OF DISTILLED SPIRITS (Proof Gallons)

ITEM	WINE SPIRITS				FOR PREPARATION OF DOSAGES OR ESSENCES (e)	DISTILLATES CONTAINING ALDEHYDES (f)	(g)	SPIRITS FOR USE IN NON BEVERAGE WINES (h)
	FOR ADDITION TO WINE							
	GRAPE (a)	(b)	(c)	(d)				
1 ON HAND BEGINNING OF PERIOD	0							
2 RECEIVED	60							
3 INVENTORY GAIN								
4 TOTAL	60							
5 USED	35							
6 TRANS TO COL. (a)								
7								
8 LOSSES								
9 ON HAND END OF PERIOD	25							
10 TOTAL	60							

PART IV - SUMMARY OF MATERIALS RECEIVED AND USED

ITEM	GRAPE MATERIAL				KINDS OF MATERIALS OTHER THAN GRAPE (Pounds or Gallons)			SUGAR	
	GRAPES		JUICE (Gallons) (c)	CONCENTRATE (Gallons) (d)	Apple Concentrate (e)	(f)	(g)	DRY (Pounds) (h)	LIQUID (Gallons) (i)
	UNCRUSHED (Pounds) (a)	FIELD CRUSHED (Gallons) (b)							
1. ON HAND BEGINNING OF PERIOD	0				0				
2. RECEIVED	500,000				200				
3. JUICE OR CONCENTRATE PRODUCED									
4. TOTAL	500,000				200				
5. USED IN WINE PRODUCTION	500,000				200				
6. USED IN JUICE OR CONCENTRATE PRODUCTION									
7. USED IN ALLIED PRODUCTS									
8. REMOVED									
9. ON HAND END OF PERIOD	0				0				
10. TOTAL	500,000				200				

PART V - (RESERVED)

PART VI - SUMMARY OF DISTILLING MATERIAL AND VINEGAR STOCK (Gallons)

ITEM	DISTILLING MATERIAL		VINEGAR STOCK	
	(a)	(b)	(c)	(d)
1 ON HAND BEGINNING OF PERIOD (Storage Tanks)				
2 PRODUCED				
3 RECEIVED FROM OTHER BONDED WINE PREMISES				
4				
5 TOTAL				
6 REMOVED TO DISTILLED SPIRITS PLANTS				
7 REMOVED TO OTHER BONDED WINE PREMISES				
8 REMOVED TO VINEGAR PLANTS				
9				
10 ON HAND END OF PERIOD (Storage Tanks)				
11 TOTAL				

PART VII - IN FERMENTERS END OF PERIOD (Gallons)

TOTAL	(a)	(b)	(c)	(d)	(e)	TOTAL
1. IN FERMENTERS (ESTIMATED QUANTITY OF LIQUID)	18,700					

PART VIII - SUMMARY OF NONBEVERAGE WINES (Gallons)

ITEM	NOT OVER 14 PERCENT ALCOHOL (a)	OVER 14 TO 21 PERCENT ALCOHOL (Inclusive) (b)	TOTAL (c)
1 PRODUCED			
2 WITHDRAWN			

PART IX - SPECIAL NATURAL WINES AND 27 CFR 24.218 WINES (Gallons)

ITEMS	VERMOUTH (a)	OTHER SPECIAL NATURAL WINES				TOTAL (cols. a, b, c, d and e) (f)	27 CFR 24.218 WINES (g)
		NOT OVER 14 PERCENT ALCOHOL (b)	OVER 14 TO 21 PERCENT ALCOHOL (c)	ARTIFICIALLY CARBONATED (d)	SPARKLING (e)		
1 PRODUCED							
2 TAXABLE REMOVALS							
3 ON HAND END OF PERIOD							

PART X - REMARKS

Under penalties of perjury I declare that I have examined this report, including the documents submitted in support thereof, and to the best of my knowledge and belief, it is true, correct, and complete.

PROPRIETOR

(Operating Name of Wine Premises)

BY (Signature and Title)

(Signer must have Power of Attorney on file with TTB)

DATE

PAPERWORK REDUCTION ACT NOTICE

This information collection request is in accordance with the Paperwork Reduction Act of 1995. The purpose of this information collection is for the protection of Federal Excise taxes. The information will be used to determine compliance by payment on untaxpaid commodities. The information required is mandatory by statute (26 U.S.C. 5314).

The estimated average burden associated with this collection of information is 1 hour and 6 minutes per respondent or recordkeeper, depending on individual circumstances. Comments concerning the accuracy of this burden estimate and suggestions for reducing this burden should be addressed to Reports Management Officer, Regulations and Procedures Division, Alcohol and Tobacco Tax and Trade Bureau, Washington, DC 20220.

An agency may not conduct or sponsor, and a person is not required to respond to, a collection of information unless it displays a currently valid OMB control number.

TTB F 5120.17 (5/2006)

Explanation of Entries on Sample "Report of Wine Premises Operations"

Section A – Bulk Wine
Line:
1) These figures were carried forward from Line 31 of previous report.

2) Winemaker moved 22,600 total gallons grape wine from primary fermentation, racked, treated with bentonite, and placed in storage tanks, and 1,200 gallons of hard cider. This wine is declared "Produced."

(Note reverse, Part VII: 18,700 gallons (estimate) is still in fermentation at the end of October. Part IV shows 200 gallons apple concentrate received and used in production.)

4) 325 gallons 14-21% alcohol port produced by wine spirits addition. The amount shown as "produced" in Column (b) Line 4 is equal to the amount "used" for wine spirits addition in Column (a) Line 19 and Part III, Column (a) Line 5 on the reverse of the report (35 gallons of 140 proof wine spirits = 25 wine gallons).

5) This winery produced 230 gallons of Angelica by blending 115 gallons of dry white wine with 115 gallons of higher alcohol wine. For purposes of the report, "blending" means blending of tax classes. Notice the components equal the whole.

7) Winery received a shipment of 600 gallons of wine in bond from another winery, without payment of tax.

8) Winemaker discovered that some bottled wine is undergoing secondary fermentation. Some of this wine was returned from the trade as unmerchantable (25 cases) and the balance never left the winery (95 cases). He dumped the entire 120 cases back to bulk. These entries are necessary because the volume of bulk wine is increased, and the volume of cased goods is decreased. (120 cases X 2.37753 = 285.3 gallons)

12) This figure is the total of lines 1 through 11, the total quantity to be accounted for in bulk, and it agrees with the figure on line 32.

13) Winery bottled 1,000 cases of 750 ml during the period. Entry is the same for Section B, Line 2.

20) This winery produced 230 gallons of Angelica by blending 115 gallons of dry white wine with 115 gallons of higher alcohol wine. For purposes of the report, "blending" means blending of tax classes. Notice the components equal the whole.

31) Book figure, obtained by subtracting total of lines 13 through 30 from line 12.

32) This figure is the total of lines 13 through 31, the total quantity accounted for, and it agrees with the figure on line 12.

Section B - Bottled Wines
Line:
1) These figures were carried forward from Section B, Line 20 of the previous report.

4) Winery returned 25 cases of wine to bond after it was returned from a wholesaler as unmerchantable because of instability.

7) This figure is the total of lines 1 through 6, the total quantity to be accounted for in bottled wine, and it agrees with the figure on line 21.

8) Winery taxably removed 500 cases of dry wine for sale; 450 cases went to a wholesaler and 50 cases went to the taxpaid area at the winery. They also taxpaid 2 cases of Port.

11) Represents 3 cases of wine consumed in the tasting room. This wine is not taxable because it was used for tasting on the bonded premises.

12) Winery exported 50 cases of wine. Figure agrees with Forms 5100.11 for the

period.

20) Book figure obtained by subtracting total of lines 8 through 19.

21) This figure is the total of lines 8 through 20, the total bottled wine accounted for, and agrees with the figure on line 7.

Part IV – Summary of Materials Received and Used
Winery received 250 tons of grapes during the month and used them all for production of wine. Line 2 shows receipt of 500,000 pounds, and line 5 shows its use in wine production. Note also that 4 and line 10 agree.

Winery received 200 gallons of apple concentrate which was used for the production of hard cider.

Part VII – In Fermenters End of Period
An estimated 18,700 gallons of materials remain in fermenters at the end of the period.

How to Begin Using the Pay.gov System

Step 1: You will need to obtain a User ID and password by filling out the Pay.gov User Agreement at:

    http://ttb.gov/epayment/user_agreement.pdf

Step 2: Mail the completed form to:

    Alcohol and Tobacco Tax and Trade Bureau
    Attention: Pay.gov
    550 Main Street, Room 8002
    Cincinnati, OH 45202

Step 3: TTB will verify that you have "signature authority" or "Power of Attorney" and issue you a User ID via e-mail. Shortly after you receive your User ID, the system administrator will contact you with your initial password. With your User ID and password, you then connect via the TTB website at:

    http://www.ttb.gov/epayment/epayment.shtml

If you need help:

For assistance in completing the User Agreement, or if you have questions about Pay.gov, please contact us:

By mail: Alcohol and Tobacco Tax and Trade Bureau
  Attention: Pay.gov
           550 Main Street, Rom 8002
  Cincinnati,   OH 45202

By telephone: 1-877-TTB-FAQS   (1-877-882-3277)

By e-mail: Pay.gov@ttb.gov

DEPARTMENT OF THE TREASURY
Alcohol and Tobacco Tax and Trade Bureau

Industry Circular 2004-4
Date: September 21, 2004

Guidelines for Submitting Operational Reports

To: Distilled Spirits Plants, Wineries, Breweries, Specially Denatured Spirits Users, Alcohol Fuel Plants, and Tobacco Manufacturers

What is the purpose of this industry circular?

This circular announces that the Alcohol and Tobacco Tax and Trade Bureau (TTB) is implementing new guidelines for the submission of operational reports by regulated industry members. TTB is taking this action to ensure the consistency of the format of the data reported. TTB also is rescinding all existing approved alternate versions of these reports and is providing guidelines describing the requirements for new alternate versions submitted for its consideration. In addition, this circular announces new requirements for filing amended operational reports with TTB in any format.

What operational report forms are affected by this announcement?

Distilled Spirits Reports:

Monthly Report of Storage Operations	TTB F 5110.11
Monthly Report of Processing Operations	TTB F 5110.28
Monthly Report of Production Operations	TTB F 5110.40
Monthly Report of Processing (Denaturing) Operations	TTB F 5110.43
User's Report of Denatured Spirits	TTB F 5150.18
Alcohol Fuel Producers Report	TTB F 5110.75

Wine Reports:

Report of Wine Premises Operations	TTB F 5120.17

Beer Reports:

Brewer's Reports of Operations	TTB F 5130.9
Brewpub Report of Operations	TTB F 5130.26

Tobacco Reports:

Monthly Report – Export Warehouse Proprietor	TTB F 5220.4
Monthly Report – Tobacco Products Importer	TTB F 5220.6
Monthly Report – Manufacturer of Tobacco Products	TTB F 5210.5

Why are these new guidelines being implemented?

TTB is now using a new computer system, the Integrated Revenue Information System (IRIS), which requires that periodic operational report forms comply with the guidelines listed below. Federal regulations provide for TTB to approve alternate methods or procedures where an industry member demonstrates that the alternate provides equivalent protection to the revenue and is not contrary to law. In the past, numerous industry members have requested endorsement of alternate methods for preparing periodic operational reports. These approved alternative versions of the operational report forms often included deleted or added lines and columns or other significant changes to the format of the reports. Many of these changes have created data entry problems, the need for many manual corrections of errors, and explanation of vague entries. As TTB works to minimize data entry problems, greater format consistency for the data provided by industry members is required.

Previously, I obtained TTB's approval to use an alternate version of an operational report form. May I continue to use my alternate version of the report form?

No; we are rescinding all earlier approvals of alternate method requests to use modified operational report forms since many of the modified forms are not compatible with the new IRIS computer system and have created an administrative burden for our agency.

May I obtain TTB's approval to use a new alternate version of an operational report form, or approval to continue using the alternate version I use now?

Yes; you may obtain our approval of an alternate method that allows for the use of a modified operational report form. However, for consistency and accuracy of data transcription, any modified report form you submit must present the required information exactly as shown on the official form (i.e. columns and rows must be arranged exactly as they are on the official form). Most of the requests we receive to use a modified form are for approval to generate reports from an automated database or spreadsheet program. Such printouts also must match the official TTB forms or we will not approve the request.

What TTB guidelines for the preparation of periodic operational report forms does this circular announce?

> (1) You must use the actual TTB operational report forms or a modified form approved by TTB that matches the format of the actual TTB form. You may not change any of the column headings or row titles on the official TTB forms, and you cannot insert additional lines or columns. If you have something different to report, you must use the appropriate "other" lines on the form.
>
> (2) All reports must contain the reporting period month and year, registry number, name, and address of your premises exactly as they appear on your approved permit/notice. Also, please enter your Employer Identification Number (EIN) on the report.
>
> (3) If you need to file an amended report, you must complete all lines on the amended operational report form. You must fill in each applicable line on the new, amended form even if you are not amending that particular line from the original report.

(4) You must complete all "Total" lines.

(5) You may not use negative figures in any block.

(6) All "on hand beginning of period" figures must match the prior reporting period's "on hand end of period" figures.

(7) The individual signing the report must have signing authority or a Power of Attorney on file with TTB's National Revenue Center.

Is there another method available to me for filing operational reports?

Yes; TTB has recently implemented the TTB Pay.gov Program (http://www.ttb.gov/epayment/epayment.shtml), which provides for online electronic submission of operational reports, tax returns, and payments. This method eliminates the need for paper submissions and allows for a more accurate, timely, and cost efficient submission by industry members and processing of the data by TTB

Who can answer my questions about filing operational reports?

If you have questions about filing your operational report forms, you may contact us via e-mail at ttbquestions@ttb.gov , or by telephone at 1-877-882-3277. You may also write to the National Revenue Center at 550 Main Street, Suite 8002, Cincinnati, OH 45202.

Arthur J. Libertucci
Administrator
Alcohol and Tobacco Tax and Trade Bureau

DEPARTMENT OF THE TREASURY
Alcohol and Tobacco Tax and Trade Bureau
<u>Industry Circular 2004-2</u>
Date: August 4, 2004

Using <u>Pay.gov</u> to Submit Alcohol and Tobacco Excise Tax Returns, Tax Payments, and Operational Reports

To: Distilled Spirits Plants, Breweries, Wineries, Tobacco Manufacturers, and Others in the Alcohol and Tobacco Production and Storage Industries.

What is the purpose of this circular?
In this circular, the Alcohol and Tobacco Tax and Trade Bureau (TTB) announces that alcohol and tobacco industry members may now electronically file Federal excise tax returns and payments through the Financial Management Service's (FMS) "Pay.gov" system. Industry members may also file certain industry operational reports through the Pay.gov system using electronic forms and signatures as described in Title 27 CFR, Part 73, Electronic Signatures; Electronic Submission of Forms.

What forms can you file through the Pay.gov system?
Through Pay.gov you can electronically create and submit the following forms:

TTB F 5000.24, Excise Tax Return (Alcohol and Tobacco) and payments;
TTB F 5210.5, Report—Manufacturer of Tobacco Products or Cigarette Papers and Tubes;
TTB F 5130.9, Brewer's Report of Operations;
TTB F 5130.26, Brewpub Report of Operations;
TTB F 5120.17, Report of Wine Premises Operations; and
TTB F 5110.11, Monthly Report of Storage Operations.

In the future, we will make operational reports for other regulated industries available through the Pay.gov system.

How will the Pay.gov system accept payments?
Pay.gov users will submit payments electronically to the Federal Reserve Bank via the automated clearinghouse (ACH) and the Federal Reserve's Fedwire funds transfer system (Fedwire).

ACH is an electronic payments network that enables the processing of debit and credit payments between financial institutions. Users input transactions into the Pay.gov system using account number and routing number information.

Fedwire is a high-speed, real-time electronic funds transfer payment mechanism that links commercial banks with the Federal Reserve Bank. With Fedwire, you ask your bank to send the payment (it is sent by a data transfer) to the appropriate Federal Reserve Bank.

For more information, please see the Federal Reserve Payment Systems Web site at http://www.federalreserve.gov/paymentsys.htm and TTB Procedure 91–1, Payment of Tax by Electronic Fund Transfer, at http://www.ttb.gov/procedures/91-1.shtml

How can I be assured that my Pay.gov excise tax payment is received to avoid penalties and interest for late filing and payment?

Your Pay.gov payment must be received by the established due date outlined in the following Alcohol and Tobacco Due Dates chart:

Semi-monthly Tax Return & Payment Due Dates for 2004:

NOTE: SEE CURRENT YEAR'S EXCISE TAX CALENDAR ON www.ttb.gov

Please Note: The above chart takes all Federal holidays into account. Under the law, State legal holidays in the State where we require you to send your excise tax payments may affect the above due dates. State legal holidays in the State where your business is headquartered DO NOT change the above due dates.

1. *For Non-EFT payers:* In the event that the due date indicated in this schedule falls on a legal State holiday in the State where we require you to make your excise tax payments, the due date is the immediately preceding date that is not a Saturday, Sunday, or legal holiday.

2. *For EFT payers:* New York State legal holidays do not advance the due date of EFT tax returns and payments as long as the Federal Reserve Bank of New York City remains open and accepts electronic fund transfer payments. If the Federal Reserve Bank of New York City is closed in observance of a New York State holiday, your EFT tax return and payment are due the preceding day the Federal Reserve Bank of New York City is open.

* Tax return periods listed for the last half of September are the result of the Uruguay Round Agreements Act, which was effective January 1, 1995. The law changed the tax return due dates for both electronic fund transfer taxpayers (EFT) and those who pay by check or money order (Non-EFT) for the month of September. Please refer to Industry Circular No. 95–4, dated July 21, 1995, for additional information.

You must submit your return and payment through Pay.gov no later than 4:00 p.m. Eastern Time one business day prior to the due date. Payment is considered received the date funds are withdrawn from your bank account, not from the date of your Pay.gov submission.

For additional information please refer to page 9 of the Pay.gov User Guide located at: http://www.ttb.gov/epayment/excise_tax_guide.pdf.

How do I begin using the Pay.gov system?
You will need to obtain a User ID and password by filling out the Pay.gov User Agreement at http://www.ttb.gov/epayment/user_agreement.pdf. Print out the completed form and mail it to:

Alcohol and Tobacco Tax and Trade Bureau, <u>Attn: Pay.gov</u>
550 Main Street - Room 8002
Cincinnati, OH 45202

We will verify the User Agreement to ensure you have either "Signature Authority" or "Power of Attorney" for the company. Then we will issue you a User ID via e-mail. Shortly after you receive your User ID, the system administrator will telephone you with your initial password. With your ID and password, you then connect via the TTB web site at
http://www.ttb.gov/epayment/epayment.shtml

For assistance in completing the User Agreement or questions about Pay.gov, please contact us. You can access the system via the TTB web site at
http://www.ttb.gov/epayment/epayment.shtml.   You may also obtain information and help at these addresses:

By mail: Alcohol and Tobacco Tax and Trade Bureau
Attn: Pay.gov
550 Main Street - Room 8002
Cincinnati, OH 45202

By Telephone: 1-877-TTB-FAQS (882-3277).

By e-mail: Pay.gov@ttb.treas.gov

Arthur J. Libertucci
Administrator
Alcohol and Tobacco Tax and Trade Bureau

Notes

OMB No. 1513-0117 (07/31/2010)

DEPARTMENT OF THE TREASURY	EFFECTIVE DATE

ALCOHOL AND TOBACCO TAX AND TRADE BUREAU (TTB)

Pay.gov User Agreement

The following constitutes the full understanding and agreement between the Alcohol and Tobacco Tax and Trade Bureau (TTB) and _____ (a person from a User Company that deals with the Alcohol and Tobacco Tax and Trade Bureau) with regard to the Pay.gov system. This system is subject to the following conditions.

1. **User Account(s) and Access:** Upon receipt of an approved agreement, the system administrator will provide a unique username to the user via email. The system administrator also will contact the user via telephone with a password that the user will be required to reset upon his/her first access of the system. With respect to the username, the following conditions apply:

   a. The user is solely responsible for the security and proper use of his/her username and password and must take all necessary steps to ensure the password is kept confidential and secure, is used properly, and is not disclosed to anyone.

   b. The user and the stated User Company agree to indemnify and hold harmless and hereby waive all potential claims for damages against the Department of Treasury and its constituent units arising from any conduct by the user, the stated User Company, and its employees or agents that results in or constitutes a breach of password security or unauthorized use of the Pay.gov system.

   c. The user and the user company agree to request revocation of the Pay.gov user ID when the user no longer has Signature Authority or Power of Attorney for the User Company.

   d. If the user or system administrator identifies that the password security has potentially been breached, they will inform each other and the system administrator will reset the password for that account and provide the new password to the user via telephone before the next tax payment due date.

   e. The user agrees he/she will use the system solely for submitting information for the stated User Company.

   f. Regardless of whether the user and the User Company have actual control over the acts of third parties, they agree that they have the last clear chance to avoid breach of password security for the username and agree to indemnify and hold TTB harmless for any such breach.

2. **Network Connection(s):** The user agrees that he/she will be responsible for providing, maintaining, and supporting a connection to the Pay.gov system via the Internet. The system administrator will be responsible for providing, maintaining, and supporting the Pay.gov system and its connection to the Internet.

3. **System Monitoring:** The user and the User Company acknowledge that the Pay.gov system is a government computer system and consents to monitoring of the system for security, system maintenance, tax administration, law enforcement, and any other purpose authorized by law.

4. **System Outage:** In the event that the user cannot access the Pay.gov system, he/she will immediately notify the system administrator to report the problem. The user and the User Company also acknowledge they still are expected to submit payments when due even if the Pay.gov system is not available.

5. **Electronic payment of taxes due:** The user and the User Company consent to the use of Automated Electronic Payments from the bank account(s) specified in the Pay.gov system for the amount(s) calculated by Pay.gov from the data entered.

6. **Confidentiality of returns and return information:** Section 6103, Title 26, United States Code prohibits the disclosure of tax return(s) or return information (as defined in Section 6103) except in specifically proscribed circumstances and provides civil and criminal penalties for the unlawful disclosure of such information. However, Section 6103 (c) permits the disclosure of return information to a designee of the taxpayer upon the taxpayer's request. The user and the User Company consent that this Agreement constitutes a request for disclosure to the User Company's designee(s) under Section 6103 (c). Further, the User Company agrees that accessing the Pay.gov system by means of the assigned username constitutes an affirmative waiver of all claims under Section 6103, Title 26 United States Code with respect to any return information transmitted during the online access session.

7. **Penalties and interest:** TTB agrees to waive penalties assessed due to failure to timely pay taxes due, where a system failure or downtime caused the delay in submission and the delay or failure to pay is not caused by error or negligence of the User Company. This limited waiver applies only to penalties for failure to pay (Section 6651 (a) (2), Title 26 United States Code), or failure to deposit (Section 6656, Title 26 United States Code), when it has been reasonably demonstrated by the User Company, to the satisfaction of TTB, that the failure to pay was caused by the downtime or failure of the Pay.gov system and not by actions of the User Company. Notwithstanding the above, the User Company understands and acknowledges that TTB lacks any legal authority to waive or compromise interest due on late or insufficient tax payments.

8. **Termination of Agreement:** TTB, the user, and the User Company agree that this User Agreement applies only to the Pay.gov system. Periodic enhancements, improvements, and changes to the Pay.gov system will not impact this agreement. Further, the user, the User Company, and TTB agree that this agreement may be terminated at any time for any reason upon written notice.

9. **Separation of conditions:** If any provision of this Agreement is held to be invalid or unenforceable for any reason whatsoever, the remaining provisions will remain valid and unimpaired, and will continue in full force and effect.

10. **Agreement:** This agreement supersedes any and all other agreements, whether oral or written, between TTB, the user, and the User Company with respect to the matters stated herein, and this agreement contains all of the covenants and agreements between the parties with respect thereto. This agreement may be amended or modified only in writing and will be effective only after affixation of the signatures of both parties' representatives.

USER INFORMATION:

NAME _____   SIGNATURE _____

TITLE _____   DATE _____

E-MAIL ADDRESS _____   TELEPHONE NUMBER _____

For Alcohol and Tobacco Companies:

I HAVE:
- [ ] SIGNATURE AUTHORITY
- [ ] BLANKET POWER OF ATTORNEY
- [ ] POWER OF ATTORNEY TO SUBMIT EXCISE TAX
- [ ] POWER OF ATTORNEY TO SUBMIT OPERATIONAL REPORTS

TTB F 5000.31 (09/2007)

COMPANY NAME

TAXPAYER IDENTIFICATION NUMBER

PERMIT / REGISTRY NUMBER(S)

ADDRESS

PERMIT / REGISTRY NUMBER(S)

ADDRESS

COMPANY NAME

TAXPAYER IDENTIFICATION NUMBER

PERMIT / REGISTRY NUMBER(S)

ADDRESS

PERMIT / REGISTRY NUMBER(S)

ADDRESS

COMPANY NAME

TAXPAYER IDENTIFICATION NUMBER

PERMIT / REGISTRY NUMBER(S)

ADDRESS

PERMIT / REGISTRY NUMBER(S)

ADDRESS

COMPANY NAME

TAXPAYER IDENTIFICATION NUMBER

PERMIT / REGISTRY NUMBER(S)

ADDRESS

PERMIT / REGISTRY NUMBER(S)

ADDRESS

COMPANY NAME

TAXPAYER IDENTIFICATION NUMBER

PERMIT / REGISTRY NUMBER(S)

ADDRESS

PERMIT / REGISTRY NUMBER(S)

ADDRESS

COMPANY NAME

TAXPAYER IDENTIFICATION NUMBER

PERMIT / REGISTRY NUMBER(S)

ADDRESS

PERMIT / REGISTRY NUMBER(S)

ADDRESS

(Please use as many copies of this page as necessary.)

TTB F 5000.31 (09/2007)

Definitions:

1. <u>Agreement</u>: This written agreement between TTB and the User.
2. <u>Automated Electronic Payments</u>: A Payment by electronic funds transfer using the Automated Clearing House payment system.
3. <u>Internal Revenue Code</u>: Title 26, United States Code
4. <u>Internet</u>: The global computer network comprising interconnected networks using standard protocols.
5. <u>Password</u>: The verification used by the Pay.gov system to permit access by an identified username.
6. <u>Pay.gov</u>: The government's electronic payment system running on a computer connected to the Internet to process and submit forms.
7. <u>System Access Request Form</u>: A form prescribed by TTB for gathering personal identification data with regard to each individual authorized to act on behalf of the User Company in the use of the Pay.gov system.
8. <u>Username</u>: The identification used to determine authorization, authority, and privileges for use of the Pay.gov system by the individual to whom access permission has been granted.
9. <u>User</u>: Person with Signature authority who will enter data into the Pay.gov system for a User Company. Note: Users may enter data for multiple User Companies.
10. <u>User Company</u>: Entity that has dealings with the Alcohol and Tobacco Tax and Trade Bureau.

------------------------------ TTB USE ONLY ------------------------------

TTB Official(s) Approval

_____   _____
SIGNATURE   SIGNATURE

_____   _____
NAME   NAME

Director, National Revenue Center   Branch Chief, National Revenue Center
TITLE   TITLE

_____   _____
DATE   DATE

PAPERWORK REDUCTION ACT NOTICE

This request is In accordance with the Paperwork Reduction Act of 1995. We use this information collection to identify, validate, approve, and register qualified users to allow for submission of electronic forms using the Pay.gov system. The information we request is voluntary but is required for enrollment in this program.

We estimate the average burden associated with this collection of information is 5 minutes per respondent or recordkeeper, depending on your individual circumstances. Address your comments concerning the accuracy of this burden estimate and suggestions to reduce this burden to the Reports Management Officer, Regulations and Rulings Division, Alcohol and Tobacco Tax and Trade Bureau, Washington, DC 20220.

An agency may not conduct or sponsor, and an individual is not required to respond to, a collection of information unless it displays a current, valid OMB control number.

PRIVACY ACT STATEMENT

We provide this information to comply with Section 3 of the Privacy Act of 1974 (5 U.S.C. 552(a)(e)(3)).

We request this information under the authority of 27 CFR Chapter 1 Part 73 Subpart C, and 26 U.S.C.- 6011, 6061, and 7502. The information requested is used to identify, validate, approve, and register qualified users to allow for submission of electronic forms using the Pay.gov System.

We use this information to make determinations for the purposes described in paragraph 2. Also we may disclose the information to other Federal, State, foreign, and local law enforcement and regulatory agency personnel to verify information on the form where law does not prohibit such disclosure. We may disclose the information to the Justice Department if it appears that the furnishing of false information may constitute a violation of Federal law. Finally, we may disclose the information to members of the public in order to verify information on the form where law does not prohibit such disclosure.

If you fail to supply complete information, there will be a delay in our approval of your participation in this program.

TTB F 5000.31 (09/2007)

Common Compliance Concerns

Listed below are a number of common problem areas found at bonded wine premises. This list is NOT intended to be all-inclusive.

Applications, Amendments, Changes
- Unreported changes of ownership, control, company principals
- Inadequate bond coverage
- Unauthorized signatures on documents
- Wine operations conducted on non-bonded premises
- Unreported change in method used to segregate taxpaid from untaxpaid wine

Alternations, Custom Crush and Home Winemakers' Centers
- An Alternating Proprietor conducts another Alternating Proprietor's wine operations
- Custom Crush client conducts unauthorized wine operations
- Unauthoriz ed distilled spirits or brewing operations take place on wine premises
- Home winemaking operations take place on bonded wine premises

Taxes

Taxable Removals

- Alcohol Content is not stated on taxable removal record
- Amount removed in each tax class is not totaled on taxable removal record
- In-Bond Removals are not totaled separately on transfer in bond record
- Daily Taxpaid Removals are not summarized daily by tax class to the nearest 10th gallon

Untaxpaid Removals

- Incomplete Transfer in Bond document, missing items such as the Registry
- Number and Address of Receiver, Alcohol Content or Tax Class
- Insufficient evidence of removals for tasting, testing, and breakage.
- Late-filed and insufficient Export documentation

Tax Returns & Small Producer Tax Credit

- Taxes are not filed on time
- Taxes paid do not match the taxable removals shown on Form 5120.17
- Use of Credit by ineligible companies
- Use of Credit beyond the 100,000 gallon annual limit
- Wrong amount of Credit used

Common Compliance Concerns, continued

Labeling
- COLAs don't match the labels
- Wine is labeled in the wrong tax class
- Records are insufficient to support label claims
- "Estate Bottled" claims are unsupportable

Records
- Materials Received and Used Record lacks sufficient information to support future label claims
- Records relating to receipt and use of spirits are insufficient
- Destructions are not pre-approved by TTB and are not documented
- TTB Application File is not being maintained properly, and the information is not current and accurate

Reports
- Reports of Wine Premises Operations (F 5120.17) are not filed timely
- Entries on the Report forms do not balance
- The report contains negative entries and/or categories are crossed out
- Annual   inventory:
  - Was not taken
  - Was not signed under penalty of perjury
  - Results were not shown on the Report of Wine Premises Operations Form 5120.17
- Bottled wine shortages were not taxpaid
- Claims were not filed for excessive bulk inventory losses

Current Issues and Resources

"NPRM" means "Notice of Proposed Rulemaking"
"TD" means "Treasury Decision"

Open for Comment: See www.Regulations.gov

Awaiting Final Rule:

Drawback of Internal Revenue Taxes
http://www.ttb.gov/wine/wine-rulemaking.shtml

> TTB NPRMs #100 and 101; Comment period closed January 14, 2010. Proposed amendments to Customs and TTB regulations to state that domestic merchandise on which no tax is paid under the Internal Revenue Code may not be substituted for imported merchandise for purposes of claims for drawback of tax under the Customs laws and regulations.

Proposed Establishment or Expansion of American Viticultural Areas
http://www.ttb.gov/wine/wine_rulemaking.shtml

- Sierra Pelona Valley AVA, TTB NPRM #97; comment period closed September 18, 2009
- Russian River Valley and Northern Sonoma AVAs (expansions), TTB NPRMs #90 and #91; comment period closed December 19, 2008

Revision of the American Viticultural Area Regulations
http://www.ttb.gov/wine/wine_rulemaking.shtml

> TTB NPRM #78; Comment period closed March 20, 2008
> Proposed allowing the use of grandfathered brand names for wines made with grapes from outside the AVA; clearer instructions for submitting petitions

Serving Facts Labeling
http://www.ttb.gov/wine/wine_rulemaking.shtml

> TTB NPRMs #73 and #75; Comment period closed January 27, 2008
> Proposed a standardized panel with serving facts

Placement of Alcohol Content Statement
http://www.ttb.gov/wine/wine_rulemaking.shtml
> TTB NPRM #74; Comment period closed November 13, 2007
> Proposed that alcohol content statement could be placed on any label affixed
> to the container rather than only on brand label

Allergens Warning Statement on Labels
http://www.ttb.gov/wine/wine_rulemaking.shtml
> TTB NPRM #62; Comment period closed December 26, 2006
> Voluntary allergens statements may be placed on labels:
> See TTB-TD-53 and 27 CFR 4.32a. http://www.ttb.gov/rpd/decisions.shtml

Revision of Distilled Spirits Plant Regulations
http://www.ttb.gov/spirits/spirits-rulemaking.shtml
> TTB NPRMs #83 and #92; comment period closed February 3, 2009

In Effect:

Establishment or Expansion of American Viticultural Areas
http://www.ttb.gov/wine/wine_rulemaking.shtml

- Swan Creek AVA, North Carolina, T.D. TTB-69 eff. May 27, 2008
- Leona Valley AVA, Los Angeles County, CA, T.D. TTB-71 eff. November 28, 2008
- Paso Robles AVA (expansion), San Luis Obispo County, CA, T.D. TTB-72, eff. February 20, 2009
- Snipes Mountain AVA, Yakima County, WA, T.D. TTB-73, eff. February 20, 2009
- Haw River Valley AVA, North Carolina, T.D. TTB-74, eff. April 29, 2009
- Lake Chelan AVA, Chelan County, WA, T.D. TTB-76, eff. May 29, 2009
- Upper Mississippi River Valley AVA, Upper Midwest States, T.D. TTB-77, eff. July 22, 2009
- Happy Canyon of Santa Barbara AVA, Santa Barbara County, CA, T.D. TTB-82, eff. November 9, 2009
- Calistoga AVA, Napa County, CA, T.D. TTB-83, eff. January 7, 2010

Notice of Proposed Rulemaking Withdrawn
http://www.ttb.gov/wine/wine_rulemaking.shtml

- Paso Robles Westside AVA, TTB Notice #94: TTB NPRM #71 withdrawn as of 4/30/09
- Tulocay AVA, TTB Notice #84: TTB NPRM #68 withdrawn as of 6/19/08

Liquor Dealer Recordkeeping and Registration, and Repeal of Certain Special (Occupational) Taxes
http://www.ttb.gov/rpd/decisions.shtml
>T.D. TTB-79 Temporary Rule and Proposed Rule, eff. 7/28/2009 through 7/30/2010

Certificate of Analysis on Imported Wine
http://www.ttb.gov/rpd/decisions.shtml
>Adopts as final rule the certification requirements regarding production practices and procedures for imported natural wine, adopted in the Miscellaneous Trade and Technical Corrections Act of 2004 as an amendment to 26 USC 5382.
>T.D. TTB-70 eff. 5/28/08

Impact of the US/EU Wine Agreement on Certificates of Label Approval for Wine Labels with a Semi-Generic Name or Retsina
http://www.ttb.gov/agreements/us_ec_wine_agreement.shtml
>Law changed on December 20, 2006.
>No new labels using the Semi-Generic Names or Retsina will be approved.
>Only "grandfathered" labels may be used.

Direct to Consumer Shipping
http://www.ttb.gov/rulings/2000-1.htm
Webb-Kenyon   Act ATF Ruling 2000-1.
>Wine Institute Guidance   www.wineinstitute.org

Bioterrorism Act – Public Law 107-188
http://www.fda.gov/oc/bioterrorism/bioact.html
>Food and Drug Administration has inspection and detention authority.
>Recordkeeping requirements in place for most wineries as of December 11, 2006.

###